sensational smoothies & drinks

Publications International, Ltd.

Favorite Brand Name Recipes at www.fbnr.com

Pictured on the front cover *(left to right):* Sparkling Strawberry Float *(page 78)* and Cantaloupe Smoothie *(page 158).*
Pictured on the front jacket flap: Chipotle Chili-Spiked Mocha Slush *(page 32).*
Pictured on the back cover: Carrot Cake Smoothie *(page 148).*

ISBN-13: 978-1-4127-1669-7
ISBN-10: 1-4127-1669-1

Library of Congress Control Number: 2008932044

Manufactured in China.

8 7 6 5 4 3 2 1

Microwave Cooking: Microwave ovens vary in wattage. Use the cooking times as guidelines and check for doneness before adding more time.

Preparation/Cooking Times: Preparation times are based on the approximate amount of time required to assemble the recipe before cooking, baking, chilling or serving. These times include preparation steps such as measuring, chopping and mixing. The fact that some preparations and cooking can be done simultaneously is taken into account. Preparation of optional ingredients and serving suggestions is not included.

Table of Contents

Tea Fusions 4

Coffee Combos 30

Chocolate Delights 44

Berry Blends 70

Citrus Sensations 104

Fruity Favorites 132

Tropical Treasures 172

Party Potions 198

Holiday Specials 218

Drink Mixes 232

Acknowledgments 248

Index 249

Tea
fusions

melon bubble tea

(pictured on page 5)

2 cups hot green tea

$\frac{1}{3}$ cup sugar

4 cups water

$\frac{1}{2}$ cup black or pastel tapioca pearls*

4 cups cubed melon (cantaloupe, honeydew or watermelon)

4 cups ice cubes

2 cups orange juice

$\frac{1}{2}$ cup unsweetened canned coconut milk

Large diameter straws* (optional)

Large, specialty tapioca pearls and straws specifically designed for bubble teas are available in Asian markets and gourmet food stores.

1. Combine green tea and sugar; stir to dissolve. Set aside.

2. Bring water to a boil in medium saucepan over high heat; add tapioca pearls. Stir gently; let pearls float to top. Reduce heat to low; simmer, uncovered, 25 minutes. Remove from heat; let stand in water 25 minutes or until pearls are chewy and translucent. Drain and rinse under cold water. Combine pearls and sweetened tea in glass pitcher; refrigerate.

3. Working in batches, place melon, ice cubes, orange juice and coconut milk in blender. Blend until smooth.

4. Place $\frac{1}{4}$ cup tapioca mixture in bottom of large glass. Fill with melon mixture. Serve with straws, if desired. *Makes 5 to 6 servings*

icy fruit tea

Concentrate
- 4 tea bags
- 1 cup boiling water
- $\frac{1}{2}$ cup honey
- $\frac{1}{4}$ cup crushed packed fresh mint leaves
- 1 cup orange juice
- $\frac{3}{4}$ cup pineapple juice
- $\frac{1}{4}$ cup fresh lime juice

Mixer
- Ice cubes
- $1\frac{1}{2}$ quarts carbonated water

1. For concentrate, place tea bags in medium bowl. Add boiling water and steep 10 minutes. Remove tea bags. Add honey and mint; mix well. Mix fruit juices in 1-quart container. Add tea mixture and refrigerate until ready to use.

2. For tea, fill 12-ounce glass with ice cubes. Add $\frac{1}{2}$ cup tea concentrate and fill glass with carbonated water.

Makes 6 servings

Tip: Garnish with a pineapple spear and mint sprig.

Favorite recipe from **National Honey Board**

Black and green teas are used most often in tea-based drinks. For new flavors of smoothies and drinks, experiment with a variety of flavored teas. Hibiscus tea adds a touch of sweetness and fabulous red color to any drink. Jasmine tea adds floral notes. Or use your favorite spiced or herbal tea along with your favorite fruit juice to create a fabulous signature beverage of your very own.

almond milk tea with tapioca

$3\frac{1}{2}$ cups water
2 black tea bags
4 teaspoons sugar
$\frac{1}{4}$ teaspoon almond extract
1 tablespoon instant tapioca
4 tablespoons milk
Ice cubes

1. Bring water to a boil in medium saucepan over high heat.

2. Pour 2 cups boiling water over tea bags in teapot or 2-cup heatproof measuring cup. Steep tea 4 minutes or until very dark. Remove tea bags; discard. Stir in sugar and almond extract; cool to room temperature.

3. Meanwhile, add tapioca to remaining $1\frac{1}{2}$ cups boiling water; boil 3 to 4 minutes over medium-high heat until tapioca is translucent and cooked through. Drain tapioca; rinse under cold water until cool.

4. Divide tapioca between 2 tall glasses; pour 2 tablespoons milk into each glass. Fill each glass three-fourths full with ice. Divide tea between glasses; stir to combine. Serve immediately. *Makes 2 (10-ounce) servings*

Variations: Substitute your favorite herbal or fruit-flavored tea for the black tea or try substituting vanilla for the almond extract.

ginger-lime iced green tea

(pictured at right)

1 quart water
2 thin slices fresh ginger (about 1 inch in diameter)
4 green tea bags
$\frac{1}{2}$ cup sugar, divided
$\frac{1}{4}$ cup freshly squeezed lime juice (2 to 3 limes)
    Ice cubes
    Sugared lime slices (optional)

1. Bring water and ginger to a boil in large saucepan. Pour water over tea bags in teapot or 4-cup heatproof measuring cup; steep 3 minutes. Remove tea bags and ginger; discard. Stir in $\frac{1}{4}$ cup sugar; cool to room temperature.

2. Mix remaining $\frac{1}{4}$ cup sugar with lime juice; add to tea. Pour tea into 4 ice-filled glasses. Garnish with lime slices.　　　*Makes 4 servings*

cranberry 'n' lemon tea punch

3 cups boiling water
6 tea bags
$\frac{1}{2}$ cup sugar
3 cups cranberry juice cocktail
$\frac{3}{4}$ cup freshly squeezed lemon juice (juice of 4 to 5 SUNKIST® lemons)
    Ice cubes

In large pitcher, pour boiling water over tea bags. Cover and steep 5 minutes. Remove tea bags. Stir in sugar. Add cranberry and lemon juices; chill. Serve over ice. Garnish with lemon peel twists, if desired.

Makes 7 (8-ounce) servings

thai coconut iced tea

(pictured at right)

2 jasmine tea bags
2 cups boiling water
1 cup unsweetened canned coconut milk
2 packets *or* 2 tablespoons sugar substitute

1. Brew 2 cups jasmine tea with boiling water according to package directions; cool to room temperature.

2. Pour ½ cup coconut milk into each glass. Stir 1 packet of sweetener into each glass until dissolved. Add ice; carefully pour half of tea into each glass. Serve immediately. *Makes 2 servings*

Tip: For a more dramatic presentation, gently pour tea over the back of a spoon held close to the surface of the coconut milk in each glass. The tea will pool in a layer on the coconut milk before blending.

tea colada

1 cup boiling water
2 LIPTON® Orange Herbal Tea Bags
1 can (8 ounces) crushed pineapple, in natural juice
1 small banana
1 tablespoon honey
1 cup ice cubes (about 6 to 8)

In teapot, pour boiling water over Lipton Orange Herbal Tea Bags; cover and brew 5 minutes. Cool.

In blender, combine tea, pineapple, banana, honey and ice cubes. Process until smooth. Serve in tall glasses, garnished, if desired, with fresh pineapple wedges. *Makes 3 (8-ounces) servings*

mint-green tea coolers

(pictured at right)

2 green tea bags
4 thin slices fresh ginger (about 1 inch in diameter)
7 or 8 large fresh mint leaves, roughly torn
2 cups boiling water
2 cups crushed ice

1. Place tea bags, ginger and mint leaves in teapot or 2-cup heatproof measuring cup. Add boiling water; steep 4 minutes. Remove tea bags, ginger and mint leaves; discard. Cool tea to room temperature.

2. Pour 1 cup crushed ice into each of 2 tall glasses. Divide tea between glasses.   *Makes 2 servings*

Tip: Squeeze a lime wedge (about $\frac{1}{8}$ of a lime) into each cooler before serving.

vanilla caramel truffle latte

1 cup water
1 cup milk
2 cinnamon sticks
3 LIPTON® Vanilla Caramel Truffle Pyramid Tea Bags
2 tablespoons sugar

In 1-quart saucepan, bring water, milk and cinnamon just to a boil. Remove from heat and add LIPTON® Vanilla Caramel Truffle Pyramid Tea Bags. Brew 3 minutes; remove Tea Bags and squeeze, then cinnamon. Stir in sugar and serve immediately.   *Makes 2 servings*

Prep Time: **15 minutes**
Brew Time: **3 minutes**

iced almond chai tea latte

(pictured at right)

4 chai tea bags
1½ cups boiling water
1 teaspoon sugar
2 tablespoons half-and-half or milk
¼ teaspoon almond extract
Whipped cream
1 teaspoon sliced almonds
⅛ teaspoon ground nutmeg
Ice cubes

1. Place tea bags in teapot or 4-cup heatproof measuring cup. Pour boiling water over tea bags; add sugar. Without removing tea bags, set aside and cool to room temperature.

2. Remove tea bags. Stir in half-and-half and almond extract. Fill 2 tall glasses with ice. Divide tea mixture between glasses. Garnish with dollop of whipped cream; top with almonds and nutmeg.   *Makes 2 servings*

hot spiced tea

4 cups freshly brewed tea
¼ cup honey
4 cinnamon sticks
4 whole cloves
4 lemon or orange slices (optional)

1. Combine tea, honey, cinnamon sticks and cloves in large saucepan; simmer 5 minutes.

2. Serve hot. Garnish with lemon slices, if desired.   *Makes 4 cups*

Favorite recipe from **National Honey Board**

orange iced tea

(pictured at right)

2 SUNKIST® oranges
4 cups boiling water
5 tea bags
  Ice cubes
  Honey or brown sugar to taste

With vegetable peeler, peel each orange in continuous spiral, removing only outer colored layer of peel (eat peeled fruit or save for other uses). In large pitcher, pour boiling water over tea bags and orange peel. Cover and steep 5 minutes. Remove tea bags; chill tea mixture with peel in covered container. To serve, remove peel and pour over ice cubes in tall glasses. Sweeten to taste with honey. Garnish with orange quarter-cartwheel slices and fresh mint leaves, if desired. *Makes 4 (8-ounce) servings*

lemon herbal iced tea

(pictured at right)

2 SUNKIST® lemons
4 cups boiling water
6 herbal tea bags (peppermint and spearmint blend or ginger-flavored)
  Ice cubes
  Honey or sugar to taste

With vegetable peeler, peel each lemon in continuous spiral, removing only outer colored layer of peel (save peeled fruit for other uses). In large pitcher, pour boiling water over tea bags and lemon peel. Cover and steep 10 minutes. Remove tea bags; chill tea mixture with peel in covered container. To serve, remove peel and pour over ice cubes in tall glasses. Sweeten to taste with honey. Garnish with lemon half-cartwheel slices, if desired. *Makes 4 (8-ounce) servings*

chai tea

2 quarts (8 cups) water
8 black tea bags
¾ cup sugar*
16 whole cloves
16 whole cardamom seeds, pods removed (optional)
5 cinnamon sticks
8 slices fresh ginger
1 cup milk

Chai tea is typically a sweet drink. For less sweet tea, reduce sugar to ½ cup.

Slow Cooker Directions

1. Combine water, tea bags, sugar, cloves, cardamom, cinnamon sticks and ginger in slow cooker. Cover; cook on HIGH 2 to 2½ hours.

2. Strain mixture; discard solids. (At this point, tea may be covered and refrigerated up to 3 days).

3. Stir in milk just before serving. Serve warm or chilled.

Makes 8 to 10 servings

Prep Time: **8 minutes**
Cook Time: **2 to 2½ hours (HIGH)**

Fresh ginger adds delicious flavor to both hot and cold beverages. Either add thin ginger slices to tea or hot liquid while steeping, or add freshly grated ginger to a cold blender drink. To keep fresh ginger on hand for making beverages, tightly wrap unpeeled ginger and store in the refrigerator for up to 3 weeks or in the freezer for up to 6 months.

mint tea juleps

3/4 cup water
3/4 cup sugar
2/3 cup coarsely chopped fresh mint
4 cups boiling water
4 LIPTON® "Brisk" Cup Size Tea Bags

In small saucepan, bring water, sugar and mint to a boil. Cook, stirring constantly, until sugar dissolves. Remove from heat and cool.

Meanwhile, in teapot, pour boiling water over Lipton "Brisk" Cup Size Tea Bags; cover and brew 5 minutes. Remove Tea Bags; cool. To serve, strain mint syrup, then stir into brewed tea. Serve over crushed ice.

Makes 5 (8-ounces) servings

southern-style peach tea

4 cups water
4 LIPTON® "Brisk" Cup Size Tea Bags
2 cups sliced fresh peaches
2 tablespoons fresh mint leaves
3 tablespoons firmly packed brown sugar

In medium saucepan, bring water to a boil. Remove from heat and add Lipton "Brisk" Cup Size Tea Bags, peaches and mint; cover and brew 5 minutes. Remove Tea Bags. In pitcher, combine tea mixture with sugar; serve over ice.

Makes 4 (8-ounces) servings

green tea lychee frappé

1 can (15 ounces) lychees in syrup,* undrained

2 cups water

2 slices peeled fresh ginger (about 1 inch in diameter and $\frac{1}{4}$ inch thick)

3 green tea bags

Canned lychees are readily available in either the canned fruit or ethnic foods section of most large supermarkets.

1. Drain lychees, reserving syrup. Place lychees in single layer in medium resealable food storage bag; freeze. Cover syrup; refrigerate.

2. Bring water and ginger to a boil in small saucepan over medium-high heat. Pour over tea bags in teapot or 2-cup heatproof measuring cup. Steep 3 minutes. Discard ginger and tea bags. Cover tea; refrigerate until cool.

3. Place frozen lychees, chilled green tea and $\frac{1}{2}$ cup reserved syrup in blender. Blend about 20 seconds or until smooth. Serve immediately.

Makes 2 (10-ounce) servings

Note: A lychee is a subtropical fruit grown in China, Mexico and the United States. It is a small oval fruit with a rough, bright red hull. Beneath the hull is milky white flesh surrounding a single seed. The flesh is sweet and juicy. The fresh lychee is a delicacy in China. They are available fresh at Asian markets in the United States in early summer. Canned lychees are readily available. They are most often served as dessert.

mulled cranberry tea

2 black tea bags
1 cup boiling water
1 bottle (48 ounces) cranberry juice
$\frac{1}{2}$ cup dried cranberries (optional)
$\frac{1}{3}$ cup sugar
1 large lemon, cut into $\frac{1}{4}$-inch slices
4 cinnamon sticks
6 whole cloves
   Additional thin lemon slices and cinnamon sticks (optional)

Slow Cooker Directions

1. Place tea bags in slow cooker. Pour boiling water over tea bags; cover and let stand 5 minutes. Remove and discard tea bags. Stir in cranberry juice, cranberries, if desired, sugar, lemon slices, 4 cinnamon sticks and cloves. Cover; cook on LOW 2 to 3 hours or on HIGH 1 to 2 hours.

2. Remove and discard lemon slices, cinnamon sticks and cloves. Serve in warm mugs with additional lemon slices and cinnamon sticks, if desired.

Makes 8 servings

Prep Time: **10 minutes**
Cook Time: **2 to 3 hours (LOW) or 1 to 2 hours (HIGH)**

green tea citrus smoothie

(pictured at right)

4 green tea bags
1 cup boiling water
3 tablespoons sugar
3 tablespoons lemon juice
1 cup frozen lemon sorbet
4 ice cubes, plus extra for glasses
1 cup club soda, chilled
4 lemon wedges

1. Place tea bags in heatproof cup or mug. Add boiling water. Steep tea 5 minutes. Remove and discard tea bags. Stir in sugar until dissolved. Refrigerate until cold.

2. Place tea, lemon juice, lemon sorbet and 4 ice cubes in blender. Blend 30 seconds to 1 minute until mixture is frothy and ice cubes are finely ground. Stir in club soda.

3. Divide smoothie between 4 glasses. Garnish each with lemon wedge.

Makes 4 servings

mango tea frost

¼ cup LIPTON® Green Tea with Honey & Lemon Iced Tea Mix
1 can (12 ounces) mango, papaya or pear nectar
¼ cup half and half
3 cups ice cubes

In blender, add all ingredients. Process until smooth. Serve immediately.

Makes 2 servings

sparkling tangerine-cranberry green tea

(pictured at right)

2 cups green tea, chilled
1 cup freshly squeezed tangerine juice (3 to 4 tangerines)
½ cup cold cranberry juice
1 cup cold seltzer water
  Ice cubes
  Tangerine slices (optional)
  Cranberries (optional)

1. Mix tea, tangerine juice, cranberry juice and seltzer in large pitcher.

2. Serve immediately in 4 ice-filled glasses. Garnish with tangerine slices or cranberries. *Makes 4 servings*

tropical tea-mulled cider

3 cups apple juice
1 cup water
¼ teaspoon ground cinnamon
3 LIPTON® White Tea with Island Mango & Peach Flavors Pyramid
  Tea Bags

In 2-quart saucepan, bring apple juice, water and cinnamon to a boil over high heat. Remove from heat. Add LIPTON® White Tea with Island Mango & Peach Flavors Pyramid Tea Bags; cover and brew 5 minutes. Remove Tea Bags and squeeze. *Makes 4 servings*

Tip: Also great with a splash of rum!

Prep Time: **10 minutes**
Brew Time: **5 minutes**

Coffee
combos

chipotle chili-spiked mocha slush

(pictured on page 31 and front jacket flap)

1 package (1 to 1¼ ounces) instant hot chocolate mix without
   marshmallows
½ teaspoon instant coffee granules
⅛ teaspoon chipotle chili powder
⅛ teaspoon ground cinnamon
¾ cup hot water
1 cup coffee, vanilla or chocolate ice cream
⅓ cup half-and-half
   Whipped cream (optional)
   Ground cinnamon (optional)

1. Combine hot chocolate mix, coffee granules, chili powder and cinnamon in 2-cup heatproof measuring cup. Stir in hot water until blended. Pour into ice cube tray. Freeze until firm.

2. Place chocolate ice cubes, ice cream and half-and-half in blender. Blend until smooth. Pour into glasses. Garnish with whipped cream and cinnamon. Serve immediately.   *Makes 1½ cups or 2 (6-ounce) servings*

frosty five-spice coffee shake

⅓ cup vanilla ice cream or frozen yogurt
2 tablespoons sweetened condensed milk
1 tablespoon instant coffee powder or granules
¼ teaspoon 5-spice powder (or garam masala spice mix)
1 cup ice cubes

1. Place ice cream, milk, coffee powder, 5-spice powder and ice cubes in blender. Blend about 20 seconds or until ice is completely crushed.

2. Pour into tall glass. Serve immediately.   *Makes 1 serving*

honey coffee cooler

2 tablespoons instant coffee granules
$\frac{1}{4}$ cup boiling water
$\frac{1}{4}$ cup honey
1 cinnamon stick
$\frac{1}{4}$ cup cold water
  Ice cubes
4 cups milk

1. Dissolve coffee granules in boiling water in medium bowl; add honey and mix well. Add cinnamon stick and stir in cold water; refrigerate.

2. Fill 4 tall glasses with ice cubes. Add 3 tablespoons coffee concentrate and fill each glass with 1 cup milk.   *Makes 4 servings*

Favorite recipe from **National Honey Board**

mocha madness

6 cups strong brewed coffee
$\frac{3}{4}$ cup **EAGLE BRAND**® Sweetened Condensed Milk (**NOT** evaporated milk)
$\frac{3}{4}$ cup chocolate-flavored syrup
  Whipped cream (optional)
  Chocolate shavings (optional)

1. In large saucepan, combine coffee, EAGLE BRAND® and chocolate syrup. Over low heat, cook and stir until coffee is hot.

2. Pour $1\frac{1}{4}$ cups coffee mixture into each of six 12-ounce mugs.

3. Garnish with whipped cream (optional) and chocolate shavings (optional). Serve immediately. Store leftovers covered in refrigerator.

                              Makes 6 servings

Prep Time: **10 minutes**

viennese coffee

(pictured at right)

3 cups strong freshly brewed hot coffee
3 tablespoons chocolate syrup
1 teaspoon sugar
$\frac{1}{3}$ cup whipping cream
$\frac{1}{4}$ cup crème de cacao or Irish cream liqueur (optional)
   Whipped cream (optional)
   Chocolate shavings (optional)

Slow Cooker Directions

1. Combine coffee, chocolate syrup and sugar in slow cooker. Cover; cook on LOW 2 to 2½ hours. Stir in whipping cream and crème de cacao, if desired. Cover; cook 30 minutes or until heated through.

2. Ladle coffee into coffee cups; top with whipped cream and chocolate shavings.

Makes 4 servings

mocha colada

3 ounces MR & MRS T® Piña Colada Mix
1 ounce COCO CASA® Cream of Coconut
2 ounces cold espresso (or other strong coffee)
1 cup ice
$\frac{1}{2}$ tablespoon chocolate syrup
   Chocolate covered espresso bean, for garnish

Blend first 4 ingredients in blender until slushy. Pour into tall glass and garnish with chocolate syrup and espresso bean.

Makes 1 serving

mocha cooler

(pictured at right)

   1 cup milk
$\frac{1}{4}$ cup vanilla or coffee ice cream
   1 tablespoon instant coffee granules
   1 tablespoon chocolate syrup

1. Place all ingredients in blender. Cover; process until smooth.

2. Pour into glass; serve immediately.   *Makes 1 serving*

espresso shake

$1\frac{1}{2}$ cups vanilla ice cream
   1 cup whipping cream
   1 tablespoon instant espresso powder
$\frac{1}{2}$ teaspoon vanilla

1. Combine all ingredients in blender. Blend until smooth.

2. Pour into 3 tall glasses; serve immediately.   *Makes 3 servings*

iced café latte

   1 can (12 ounces) NESTLÉ® CARNATION® Evaporated Lowfat 2% Milk
   4 to 5 teaspoons NESCAFÉ TASTER'S CHOICE 100% Pure Instant Coffee
      Granules
   3 teaspoons granulated sugar
      Ice cubes

COMBINE evaporated milk, instant coffee and sugar in 2-cup glass
measure. Microwave on HIGH (100%) power for 1 minute; stir well.
Pour over ice cubes.   *Makes 2 servings*

tiramisu smoothie

(pictured at right)

 8 ounces mascarpone cheese
$3/4$ cup vanilla frozen yogurt
$1/4$ cup half-and-half
$1^1/2$ cups chocolate frozen yogurt
$1/2$ cup brewed espresso or strong coffee, chilled
 1 tablespoon powdered sugar
 1 tablespoon cocoa powder
 Pirouette cookies or thin biscotti (optional)

1. Place mascarpone, vanilla frozen yogurt and half-and-half in blender. Blend until smooth and creamy. Scrape down sides of blender. Pour mixture into pitcher; set aside.

2. Place chocolate frozen yogurt and espresso in blender. Blend until smooth. Divide chocolate mixture among 4 glasses. Top with mascarpone mixture.

3. Mix powdered sugar and cocoa in small bowl. Sift mixture over each glass. Garnish with cookie. Serve immediately.   *Makes 4 servings*

spanish coffee

$3/4$ cup coffee-flavored liqueur
 1 tablespoon plus 1 teaspoon sugar
 4 cups hot brewed coffee
 Whipped cream
 Chocolate curls (optional)

1. Stir liqueur and sugar into hot coffee.

2. Pour into 4 heatproof glasses or mugs. Top each serving with dollop of whipped cream. Garnish with chocolate curls.   *Makes 4 servings*

chilled café latte

(pictured at right)

2 tablespoons instant coffee
$^3/_4$ cup warm water
1 (14-ounce) can EAGLE BRAND® Fat Free or Original Sweetened
    Condensed Milk (NOT evaporated milk)
1 teaspoon vanilla extract
4 cups ice cubes

1. In blender container, dissolve coffee in water. Add EAGLE BRAND® and vanilla; cover and blend on high speed until smooth.

2. With blender running, gradually add ice cubes, blending until smooth. Serve immediately. Store leftovers covered in refrigerator.

Makes about 5 cups

Prep Time: **10 minutes**

mocha shake

$^1/_4$ cup warm water
2 tablespoons HERSHEY'S Cocoa
1 tablespoon sugar
1 to 2 teaspoons powdered instant coffee
$^1/_2$ cup milk
2 cups vanilla ice cream

1. Place water, cocoa, sugar and instant coffee in blender container. Cover; blend briefly on low speed. Add milk. Cover; blend well on high speed. Add ice cream. Cover; blend until smooth.

2. Serve immediately. Garnish as desired.

Makes 3 servings

iced mexican coffee

(pictured at right)

$^1/_2$ cup ground dark roast coffee
4 cups water
1 tablespoon sugar
$^2/_3$ cup half-and-half or milk
$^1/_4$ cup chocolate syrup
1 teaspoon vanilla
$^1/_2$ teaspoon cinnamon extract*
Ice cubes

Or omit cinnamon extract and break 2 (3-inch-long) cinnamon sticks into several pieces. Place cinnamon pieces in filter basket of coffee maker with ground coffee. Continue as directed.

1. Place ground coffee in filter basket of coffee maker. Add water to coffee maker and brew according to manufacturer's directions. Discard coffee grounds. Pour coffee into 4-cup heatproof measuring cup. Add sugar; stir until dissolved. Cover; cool to room temperature.

2. Combine half-and-half, chocolate syrup, vanilla and cinnamon extract in small pitcher. Stir into cooled coffee. Serve immediately in ice-filled glasses.

Makes 4$^1/_2$ cups or 6 (6-ounce) servings

kahlúa® & coffee

1$^1/_2$ ounces KAHLÚA® Liqueur
Hot coffee
Whipped cream (optional)

Pour Kahlúa® into steaming cup of coffee. Top with whipped cream.

Makes 1 serving

Chocolate
delights

irish cream iced cappuccino

(pictured on page 45)

  1 cup water
  $\frac{1}{2}$ cup cocoa
  $\frac{1}{2}$ cup instant coffee granules
  $\frac{1}{2}$ cup EQUAL® SPOONFUL*
  6 cups fat-free milk
  $\frac{1}{2}$ cup liquid Irish cream coffee creamer

May substitute 12 packets EQUAL® sweetener.

• Whisk together first 3 ingredients in large saucepan until smooth. Bring to a boil over medium heat, whisking constantly. Boil 2 minutes, whisking constantly. Remove mixture from heat; stir in Equal®. Cool slightly.

• Whisk in milk and creamer. Cover and chill at least 4 hours or up to 2 days.

• Serve over ice.　　　　　　　　　　　　　　*Makes 8 servings*

chocolate root beer float

  1 tablespoon sugar
  2 teaspoons HERSHEY'S Cocoa
  1 tablespoon hot water
  1 scoop vanilla ice cream
    Cold root beer

1. Stir together sugar and cocoa in 12-ounce glass; stir in water.

2. Add ice cream and enough root beer to half fill glass; stir gently. Fill glass with root beer. Stir; serve immediately.　　*Makes 1 (12-ounce) serving*

peanut butter chocolate twist shake

6 ounces frozen vanilla yogurt or ice cream
$\frac{1}{2}$ cup (4 ounces) unsweetened canned coconut milk or milk
1 ounce chocolate chips
1 ounce peanut butter
2 curls shaved chocolate
$\frac{1}{2}$ ounce crushed roasted peanuts

Whip all ingredients except shaved chocolate and peanuts together in blender until smooth. Garnish with shaved chocolate and crushed roasted peanuts. *Makes 1 serving*

Favorite recipe from **Peanut Advisory Board**

chocolate covered banana slushy

3 cups milk, divided
$\frac{1}{4}$ cup chocolate instant beverage mix
1 medium banana (about 6 ounces)

1. Combine 2 cups milk and beverage mix in pitcher. Whisk until powder dissolves. Pour chocolate milk into ice cube trays. Freeze until solid.

2. Remove cubes from trays. Place in blender. Pour remaining 1 cup milk over cubes. Blend until slushy, stopping to scrape blender sides as necessary until blended.

3. Add banana. Blend until slushy. Serve immediately.

Makes 8 servings

"m&m's"® brain freezer shake

(pictured at right)

2 cups any flavor ice cream
1 cup milk
¾ cup "M&M's"® Chocolate Mini Baking Bits, divided
Aerosol whipped topping
Additional "M&M's"® Chocolate Mini Baking Bits for garnish

In blender container combine ice cream and milk; blend until smooth. Add ½ cup "M&M's"® Chocolate Mini Baking Bits; blend just until mixed. Pour into 2 glasses. Top each glass with whipped topping; sprinkle with remaining ¼ cup "M&M's"® Chocolate Mini Baking Bits. Serve immediately.

Makes 2 (1¼-cup) servings

hot chocolate tea

1 cup water
2 tablespoons sugar
2 LIPTON® Bedtime Story Caffeine-Free Herbal Pyramid Tea Bags
¾ cup chocolate soy milk

In 1-quart saucepan, bring water and sugar to a boil over high heat. Remove from heat and add LIPTON® Bedtime Story Caffeine-Free Herbal Pyramid Tea Bags; cover and brew 5 minutes. Remove Tea Bags and squeeze. Stir in soy milk and heat through.   Makes 2 servings

Variation: Also makes a great cold drink! In blender, process chilled tea, soy milk and 2 cups ice cubes until slushy. Serve immediately.

Prep Time: 10 minutes
Cook Time: 2 minutes
Brew Time: 5 minutes

creamy hot chocolate

1 (14-ounce) can EAGLE BRAND® Sweetened Condensed Milk (NOT evaporated milk)
½ cup unsweetened cocoa powder
1½ teaspoons vanilla extract
Dash salt
6½ cups water
Miniature marshmallows (optional)

1. In large saucepan over medium heat, combine EAGLE BRAND®, cocoa, vanilla and salt; mix well. Slowly stir in water. Heat through, stirring occasionally. Do not boil.

2. Top with marshmallows (optional). Store leftovers covered in refrigerator.

Makes about 8 cups

Microwave Method: In 2-quart glass measure, combine all ingredients except marshmallows. Microwave on HIGH (100% power) 8 to 10 minutes, stirring every 3 minutes. Top with marshmallows (optional).

Prep Time: 8 to 10 minutes

Leftover Creamy Hot Chocolate can be stored in the refrigerator for up to 5 days. Mix well and reheat before serving.

"hot" chocolate smoothie

(pictured at right)

2½ cups chocolate frozen yogurt
1¾ cups chocolate soy milk
1 banana
⅛ teaspoon chipotle chili powder
1½ cups ice
Chocolate shavings (optional)

1. Place frozen yogurt, soy milk, banana, chili powder and ice in blender. Blend until smooth, stopping once to scrape down sides.

2. Pour into 4 glasses. Top with chocolate shavings, if desired. Serve immediately. *Makes 4 servings*

strawberry & chocolate shake

¼ cup sugar
3 tablespoons HERSHEY'S Cocoa
¼ cup water
½ cup cold milk
1½ cups sliced fresh strawberries
1 teaspoon vanilla extract
2 cups (1 pint) vanilla ice cream

1. Stir together sugar and cocoa in small microwave-safe bowl; stir in water. Microwave at MEDIUM (50%) 30 to 45 seconds until hot; stir until sugar is dissolved. Cool to room temperature. Place cocoa mixture, milk, strawberries and vanilla in blender container. Cover; blend well.

2. Add ice cream. Cover; blend until smooth. Serve immediately.
Makes 5 servings

egg cream

(pictured at right)

$1/2$ cup half-and-half, divided
2 tablespoons chocolate syrup, divided
2 cups unsweetened seltzer water or club soda, chilled

Pour $1/4$ cup half-and-half into each of two tall glasses; stir 1 tablespoon chocolate syrup into each. Add 1 cup seltzer to each glass.

Makes 2 servings

black pearl hot 'n spicy chocolate tea

1 cup milk or half & half
1 cup water
2 LIPTON® Black Pearl Black Pyramid Tea Bags
1 tablespoon sugar or to taste
$1/8$ teaspoon ground cinnamon
$1/8$ teaspoon ground ginger
$1/8$ teaspoon ground nutmeg
1 teaspoon to 1 tablespoon chocolate syrup

In 2-quart saucepan, bring milk and water just to a boil. Remove from heat and add LIPTON® Black Pearl Black Pyramid Tea Bags. Cover and brew $1/2$ minutes. Remove Tea Bags and squeeze; stir in remaining ingredients. Serve immediately. Garnish, if desired, with whipped cream and a sprinkle of cinnamon.

Makes 2 servings

Prep Time: 5 minutes
Brew Time: 1 minute 30 seconds
Cook Time: 5 minutes

peachy chocolate yogurt shake

(pictured at right)

$2/3$ cup peeled fresh peach slices *or* 1 package (10 ounces) frozen
    peach slices, thawed and drained
$1/4$ teaspoon almond extract
  2 cups (1 pint) vanilla nonfat frozen yogurt
$1/4$ cup HERSHEY'S Syrup
$1/4$ cup nonfat milk

1. Place peaches and almond extract in blender container. Cover; blend until smooth. Add frozen yogurt, syrup and milk. Cover; blend until smooth.

2. Serve immediately.   *Makes 4 servings*

mysterious chocolate mint coolers

  2 cups milk or half-and-half
$1/4$ cup chocolate syrup
  1 teaspoon peppermint extract
    Crushed ice
    Aerosol whipped topping (optional)
    Mint leaves

1. Combine milk, chocolate syrup and peppermint extract in small pitcher; stir until well blended.

2. Fill 2 glasses with crushed ice. Pour chocolate-mint mixture over ice. Top with whipped topping, if desired. Garnish with mint leaves.
        Makes about 2 (10-ounce) servings

banana split shakes

(pictured at right)

  1 ripe banana
  $\frac{1}{4}$ cup milk
  5 maraschino cherries, drained
  1 tablespoon chocolate syrup
  $\frac{1}{8}$ teaspoon coconut extract
  4 cups chocolate frozen yogurt

1. Combine banana, milk, cherries, chocolate syrup and coconut extract in blender. Blend until smooth.

2. Add yogurt 1 cup at a time. Blend after each addition using on/off pulsing action until smooth and thick. Pour into 4 glasses. Garnish with additional maraschino cherries, if desired.   *Makes 4 servings*

Tip: For a low-fat shake, chop 3 large peeled bananas. Place in resealable plastic bag and freeze until solid. Blend with milk, cherries, chocolate syrup and coconut extract. Omit frozen yogurt.

chocolate chip cookie milk shake

  3 cups French vanilla ice cream
  2 cups milk
  $\frac{1}{2}$ cup packed brown sugar
  1 teaspoon vanilla
  2 ounces semisweet chocolate, grated

1. Place ice cream, milk, sugar and vanilla in blender. Blend about 1 minute or until smooth. Add chocolate. Blend briefly just until combined.

2. Pour shake into 4 glasses; serve immediately.   *Makes 4 servings*

Tip: Use a rotary grater with a medium wheel to easily grate chocolate.

mint chocolate chip milkshakes

(pictured at right)

2 cups mint chocolate chip ice cream
1 cup milk
2 tablespoons whipped topping
1 tablespoon mini chocolate chips

1. Combine ice cream and milk in blender; blend until smooth.

2. Pour into glasses. Top with whipped topping; sprinkle with chocolate chips.   *Makes 2 servings*

royal hot chocolate

4 sections (¹/₂ ounce each) HERSHEY⸝S Unsweetened Chocolate
    Premium Baking Bar, broken into pieces
1 can (14 ounces) sweetened condensed milk (not evaporated milk)
4 cups boiling water
1 teaspoon vanilla extract
    Dash salt
    Sweetened whipped cream (optional)
    Ground cinnamon (optional)

1. Melt chocolate in large heavy saucepan over low heat. Stir in sweetened condensed milk. Gradually add water, stirring until well blended. Stir in vanilla and salt.

2. Garnish with whipped cream and cinnamon, if desired. Serve immediately.   *Makes 8 servings*

frozen hot chocolate

½ **cup milk**

3 **tablespoons sugar**

3 **ounces finely chopped semisweet chocolate** *or* ⅔ **cup semisweet chocolate chips**

1 **tablespoon hot chocolate mix powder**

4 **scoops chocolate ice cream**

2 **cups ice cubes**

Whipped cream, chocolate sprinkles or mini marshmallows (optional)

1. Place milk, sugar, chopped chocolate and hot chocolate mix in medium microwavable bowl. Microwave on HIGH 30 seconds; stir until chocolate is melted and mixture is smooth. Cool to room temperature, about 1 hour (or refrigerate and bring to room temperature when ready to serve).

2. To serve, place chocolate mixture, ice cream and ice cubes in blender; blend until smooth. Serve in tall glasses; garnish with whipped cream and sprinkles. *Makes 3 to 4 servings*

Freeze leftover cooled hot chocolate, coffee, tea or juices in ice cube trays to use later in icy beverages. Flavored ice cubes not only help keep drinks from getting diluted but are great for making quick blender drinks like slushies or smoothies.

cherry chocolate frosty

(pictured at right)

1 container (6 ounces) chocolate yogurt
$1/2$ cup frozen dark sweet cherries
$1/8$ to $1/4$ teaspoon almond extract

1. Combine yogurt, cherries and almond extract in blender; blend about 30 seconds or until smooth.

2. Pour into glass; serve immediately. *Makes 1 ($3/4$-cup) serving*

drinking chocolate

2 sections ($1/2$ ounce each) HERSHEY˙S Unsweetened Chocolate Premium Baking Bar
2 tablespoons hot water
$1/4$ cup sugar
Dash of salt
$1/4$ cup milk, warmed
$1/4$ teaspoon vanilla extract

1. Place chocolate and water in top of small double boiler. Melt over simmering water, stirring until smooth. Stir in sugar and salt, blending thoroughly. Gradually blend in warm milk. Heat, stirring occasionally, until hot. Stir in vanilla.

2. Pour into demitasse cups. Garnish as desired. Serve immediately.
Makes 2 servings

mint-turtle tornado

(pictured at right)

1$\frac{1}{2}$ cups chocolate frozen yogurt
$\frac{3}{4}$ cup vanilla frozen yogurt
$\frac{3}{4}$ cup milk
$\frac{1}{4}$ cup caramel ice cream topping, plus extra for garnish
$\frac{1}{4}$ cup mint chocolate chips, plus extra for garnish

1. Place frozen yogurt, milk, $\frac{1}{4}$ cup caramel topping and $\frac{1}{4}$ cup mint chocolate chips in blender. Blend until smooth.

2. Pour into 4 glasses. Sprinkle additional mint chocolate chips over top of each glass. Drizzle with additional caramel topping. Serve immediately.

Makes 4 servings

raspberry chocolate smoothie

2 cups fresh or frozen raspberries
$\frac{3}{4}$ cup milk
1 container (6 ounces) vanilla yogurt
3 tablespoons chocolate syrup
1 to 3 ice cubes

1. Combine raspberries, milk, yogurt and chocolate syrup in blender. Blend until fruit is puréed and mixture is smooth. Add 3 ice cubes if using fresh fruit and 1 to 2 ice cubes if using frozen fruit. Blend until smooth.

2. Pour into 2 glasses. Serve immediately.

Makes 2 (12-ounce) servings

coconut cream pie chill

(pictured at right)

1½ cups vanilla frozen yogurt
1½ cups chocolate frozen yogurt
¾ cup unsweetened canned coconut milk
½ cup sweetened flaked coconut, divided
2 tablespoons cream of coconut
4 pineapple slices *or* 1 can (14 ounces) pineapple chunks

1. Place vanilla and chocolate frozen yogurt, coconut milk, ¼ cup flaked coconut and cream of coconut in blender. Blend until creamy.

2. Pour mixture into 4 glasses. Top each glass with 1 pineapple slice. Sprinkle with remaining ¼ cup flaked coconut. Serve immediately.

Makes 4 servings

mystic chocolate mint cooler

2 cups cold whole milk or half-and-half
¼ cup HERSHEY'S Syrup
¼ cup white crème de menthe liqueur (mint-flavored liqueur)
1 cup crushed ice

1. Combine all ingredients except crushed ice in small pitcher; stir until well blended.

2. Serve immediately over crushed ice.

Makes about 2 (10-ounce) servings

Berry

blends

cranberry lime ricky

(pictured on page 71)

6 ice cubes
$\frac{1}{2}$ cup cranberry juice
2 tablespoons grenadine
2 tablespoons lime juice
$\frac{1}{2}$ cup seltzer water

1. Place ice cubes in tall glass.

2. Pour cranberry juice, grenadine and lime juice over ice cubes. Stir until well blended. Add seltzer water. *Makes 1 (10-ounce) serving*

banana berry smoothie

1 can (14 ounces) NESTLÉ® CARNATION® Sweetened Condensed Milk
1 can (12 ounces) NESTLÉ® CARNATION® Evaporated Milk
1 ripe banana, sliced
2 cups frozen strawberries* (about half 16-ounce bag)

If frozen berries are not available, substitute with 2 cups fresh berries and 1 cup of ice cubes.

PLACE sweetened condensed milk, evaporated milk, banana and strawberries in blender; cover. Blend until smooth. *Makes 6 servings*

Prep Time: **5 minutes**

powerful pomegranate smoothie

$1\frac{1}{2}$ cups pomegranate juice
$1\frac{1}{2}$ cups strawberry sorbet
$1\frac{1}{2}$ cups sliced fresh strawberries
  2 containers (about 4 ounces each) fresh blueberries
$1\frac{1}{2}$ cups ice cubes

1. Place all ingredients in blender. Blend until smooth, stopping once to scrape down sides.

2. Serve immediately.   *Makes 5 servings*

wake-me-up breakfast smoothie

  2 containers (6 ounces each) vanilla yogurt
  2 cups sliced fresh strawberries
$1\frac{1}{2}$ cups ice cubes
  1 banana
$\frac{1}{2}$ cup milk
  2 tablespoons wheat germ
  1 tablespoon maple syrup

1. Place all ingredients in blender. Blend until smooth, stopping once to scrape down sides.

2. Divide smoothie between 6 glasses. Serve immediately.

Makes 6 servings

strawberry cheesecake smoothie

1 cup whole frozen strawberries
1 package (8 ounces) cream cheese
¾ cup vanilla frozen yogurt
¼ cup milk
¼ cup strawberry yogurt
   Graham cracker crumbs (optional)
   Fresh strawberries (optional)

1. Place strawberries, cream cheese, vanilla frozen yogurt, milk and strawberry yogurt in blender. Blend until smooth.

2. Pour mixture into 4 glasses. Sprinkle with graham cracker crumbs. Garnish with fresh strawberries. *Makes 4 servings*

To make cool creamy smoothies in minutes, use frozen fruit. Not only is the fruit washed, peeled or stemmed, but the icy fruit makes the beverage instantly thick. Freeze overripe fresh fruit instead of throwing it out. You'll not only cut down on waste but will have the ingredients on hand for instant smoothies.

bubbling raspberry coolers

(pictured at right)

$^3/_4$ cup raspberry vinegar
$^1/_2$ cup sugar
 2 liters seltzer water
   Ice cubes
 2 pints fresh raspberries
   Fresh mint leaves

1. Bring raspberry vinegar and sugar to a boil in small saucepan over medium heat. Boil, stirring frequently, 1 minute or until sugar is dissolved. Set aside to cool.

2. Place cooled syrup in large pitcher; stir in seltzer water. To serve, fill each glass with ice, a few raspberries and mint leaves. Fill glasses with raspberry mixture. Serve immediately. *Makes 8 to 10 servings*

berry berry mango smoothie

 1 medium mango, cubed (about 1 cup)
 1 cup frozen strawberries
$^1/_2$ cup frozen raspberries
$^1/_2$ cup vanilla yogurt
$^1/_2$ cup milk
 2 tablespoons honey

1. Combine all ingredients in blender. Blend until smooth, stopping once to scrape down sides.

2. Pour into 2 glasses. Serve immediately. *Makes 2 servings*

sparkling strawberry float

(pictured on the front cover)

2 tablespoons pink decorative sugar (optional)
2 cups frozen unsweetened strawberries
1 container (6 ounces) strawberry yogurt
½ cup milk
2 tablespoons honey or sugar
2 scoops strawberry sorbet

1. Place sugar in small shallow dish. Wet rims of 2 glasses with damp paper towel; dip into sugar. Place glasses upright to dry.

2. Place strawberries, yogurt, milk and honey in blender; blend until smooth. Divide between prepared glasses. Top each glass with scoop of strawberry sorbet.   *Makes 2 servings*

Prep Time: **10 minutes**

For parties and special events, serve smoothies and drinks with interesting garnishes or in decorated glasses. Dip the rims of the glasses in colored sugars, serve with sugar cane or cinnamon sticks swizzle sticks or top with a dollop of whipped cream. Citrus rounds or wedges, cookie crumbs and even a drizzle of ice cream topping are other easy garnishes that add glamour to your drinks.

raspberry peach perfection smoothie

(pictured at right)

1½ cups fresh or frozen peach slices
1 cup peach nectar
1 container (6 ounces) raspberry yogurt
¾ cup fresh or frozen raspberries
1 tablespoon honey (optional)
1 to 3 ice cubes
Fresh peach wedges and raspberries (optional)

1. Combine peaches, nectar, yogurt, raspberries and honey, if desired, in blender. Blend until fruit is puréed and mixture is smooth.

2. Add 3 ice cubes if using fresh fruit and 1 to 2 ice cubes if using frozen fruit. Blend until smooth. Pour smoothie into 2 glasses. Garnish with peach wedge and raspberries. Serve immediately.

Makes 2 (12-ounce) servings

peanut butter & jelly shakes

1½ cups vanilla ice cream
¼ cup milk
2 tablespoons creamy peanut butter
6 peanut butter sandwich cookies, coarsely chopped
¼ cup strawberry preserves

1. Place ice cream, milk and peanut butter in blender. Blend 1 to 2 minutes or until smooth. Add chopped cookies; blend 10 seconds at low speed.

2. Pour into 2 glasses. Place preserves and 1 to 2 teaspoons water in small bowl; stir until smooth. Stir 2 tablespoons preserve mixture into each glass. Serve immediately.

Makes 2 servings

Variation: Use any flavor of preserves in place of strawberry.

Prep Time: **10 minutes**

blueberry cherry "cheesecake" smoothie

(pictured at right)

2 cups fresh or frozen blueberries
1$\frac{1}{4}$ cups milk
$\frac{1}{2}$ cup fresh or frozen cherries
2 ounces ($\frac{1}{4}$ cup) cream cheese
1 to 3 ice cubes

1. Combine blueberries, milk, cherries and cream cheese in blender. Blend until mixture is smooth.

2. Add 3 ice cubes if using fresh fruit and 1 to 2 ice cubes if using frozen fruit. Blend until smooth. Pour into 2 glasses. Serve immediately.

Makes 2 (12-ounce) servings

lemon-raspberry brain freeze

$\frac{3}{4}$ cup freshly squeezed lemon juice (about 5 lemons)
$\frac{1}{2}$ cup sugar
1$\frac{1}{2}$ cups frozen raspberries, plus extra for garnish
1 cup water or seltzer water
2 cups ice
Fresh mint leaves (optional)

1. Mix lemon juice and sugar in small bowl. Stir until sugar dissolves.

2. Place lemon juice mixture, raspberries, water and ice in blender. Blend until smooth, stopping once to scrape down sides.

3. Pour mixture into 4 glasses. Garnish with raspberries and mint. Serve immediately. *Makes 4 servings*

Berry Blends

berry soy-cream blend

(pictured at right)

2 cups frozen mixed berries
1 can (14 ounces) blackberries with juice
1 cup soy milk or almond milk
1 cup apple juice
$\frac{1}{2}$ cup (4 ounces) soft tofu enriched with calcium

Place all ingredients in blender. Blend until smooth. Divide between
2 glasses; serve immediately.   *Makes 2 servings*

raspberry mint cooler

1 to 2 cups fresh mint leaves
5 cups DOLE® Pineapple Juice, chilled
2 cups DOLE® Frozen Raspberries
1 bottle (32 ounces) lemon-lime soda, chilled
1 can (6 ounces) frozen limeade concentrate, thawed
1 lime, thinly sliced for garnish (optional)

• Rub mint leaves around sides of punch bowl, then drop the bruised leaves
in bottom of bowl.

• Combine remaining ingredients in punch bowl.   *Makes 15 servings*

triple berry blast

1 cup frozen mixed berries
1 cup soy milk*
$\frac{1}{2}$ cup sliced banana
2 teaspoons honey

Do not use vanilla-flavored soy milk because it will make this smoothie too sweet.

1. Combine berries, soy milk, banana and honey in blender. Blend about 30 seconds or until smooth and thick.

2. Pour into 2 sugar-dipped glasses. Serve immediately.

Makes 2 (10-ounce) servings

Note: Soy milk is a ready-to-serve beverage often found in the refrigerated foods section near the yogurt or organic foods.

Sugar-Dipped Glasses: For a festive look and taste, add sugar to the rim of your glasses. Wet the rim with water, juice or by running a lime or lemon along the rim. Then dip the glass in decorative sugar.

Salt-Dipped Glasses: Wet the rim of your glasses with water or by running a lime or lemon along the rim. Then dip the glass in coarse or special margarita salt.

kiwi strawberry smoothie

(pictured at right)

2 kiwi, peeled and sliced
1 cup frozen whole unsweetened strawberries
1 container (6 ounces) strawberry yogurt
$\frac{1}{2}$ cup milk
2 tablespoons honey

1. Place all ingredients in blender. Blend 15 to 30 seconds or until smooth.

2. Divide between 2 glasses. Serve immediately.

Makes 2 (1-cup) servings

Soy Kiwi Strawberry Smoothie: **Substitute 1 container (6 ounces) strawberry soy yogurt for regular strawberry yogurt and $\frac{1}{2}$ cup soy milk for regular milk.**

black forest smoothie

1 container (6 ounces) dark cherry-flavored yogurt
$\frac{1}{2}$ cup frozen dark sweet cherries
$\frac{1}{4}$ cup milk
2 tablespoons sugar
2 tablespoons unsweetened cocoa powder
$\frac{1}{4}$ teaspoon almond extract
1 to 2 ice cubes

1. Place all ingredients in blender. Blend 15 to 30 seconds or until smooth.

2. Divide between 2 glasses. Serve immediately.

Makes 2 ($\frac{3}{4}$-cup) servings

raspberry soda smoothie

2 cups fresh or frozen raspberries
1 can (12 ounces) ginger ale or lemon-lime soda
1 container (6 ounces) raspberry or vanilla yogurt
1 to 3 ice cubes

1. Combine raspberries, soda and yogurt in blender. Blend until fruit is puréed and mixture is smooth.

2. Add 3 ice cubes if using fresh fruit and 1 to 2 ice cubes if using frozen fruit. Blend until smooth. Pour smoothie into 2 glasses. Serve immediately.

Makes 2 (12-ounce) servings

Variation: **For a non-dairy alternative, add ½ cup raspberry sorbet and omit yogurt and ice cubes.**

Berries are a good source of vitamins. Drinking fruit smoothies containing berries can help replenish key nutritients and keep us healthy. Berries not only mix well with most fruits but add vibrant color and incredible flavor!

blueberry pineapple smoothie

(pictured at right)

2 cups fresh or frozen blueberries
1½ cups diced pineapple
1 cup pineapple juice
1 to 3 ice cubes

1. Combine blueberries, pineapple and juice in blender. Blend until fruit is puréed and mixture is smooth.

2. Add 3 ice cubes if using fresh fruit and 1 to 2 ice cubes if using frozen fruit. Blend until smooth. Pour smoothie into 2 glasses. Serve immediately.

Makes 2 (12-ounce) servings

strawberry blast

1 package (4-serving size) strawberry gelatin
½ cup boiling water
1 container (6 ounces) strawberry yogurt
3 cups ice cubes

1. Pour gelatin and boiling water into blender. Blend until gelatin dissolves. Add yogurt; blend until mixed. Add ice cubes, 1 cup at a time, using on/off pulsing action to break up cubes after each addition.

2. Serve immediately or chill 1 hour. When chilled, the texture changes to a thicker, soft-gel texture.

Makes 4 servings

mixed berry smoothie

1½ cups fresh or frozen strawberries
1 cup fresh or frozen blueberries
1 cup apple juice
1 container (6 ounces) mixed berry or vanilla yogurt
½ cup fresh or frozen raspberries
1 to 3 ice cubes

1. Combine strawberries, blueberries, apple juice, yogurt and raspberries in blender. Blend until fruit is puréed and mixture is smooth.

2. Add 3 ice cubes if using fresh fruit and 1 to 2 ice cubes if using frozen fruit. Blend until smooth. Pour smoothie into 2 glasses. Serve immediately.

Makes 2 (12-ounce) servings

tip

When buying juices such as apple juice, grape juice or cranberry juice for drinks and smoothies, select products labeled "100 percent juice" not "juice drink" or "juice cocktail." Juice drinks and juice cocktails often have little juice and lots of additional sugar.

chocolate-blueberry soy shake

(pictured at right)

1/2 cup plus 2 tablespoons soy milk
2 tablespoons frozen or fresh blueberries
1/4 teaspoon unsweetened cocoa powder
1/4 cup crushed ice

1. Place all ingredients in blender. Blend 30 seconds or until smooth.

2. Pour into chilled glass. Serve immediately.　　　　*Makes 1 serving*

red tea harvest strawberry smoothie

1 cup boiling water
3 LIPTON® Red Tea with Harvest Strawberry & Passionfruit Flavor
　Pyramid Tea Bags
2 tablespoons sugar
1 cup frozen strawberries
1/2 cup strawberry frozen yogurt
1/2 cup ice cubes (about 3 to 4)

Pour boiling water over LIPTON® Red Tea with Harvest Strawberry
& Passionfruit Flavor Pyramid Tea Bags; cover and brew 5 minutes.
Remove Tea Bags and squeeze, then stir in sugar; chill.

In blender, process tea, strawberries and yogurt. Add ice cubes, one at a
time, and process until blended. Garnish, if desired, with whipped cream
and strawberries. Serve immediately.　　　　*Makes 2 servings*

Substitution: This recipe can also be made with regular strawberry yogurt.

Variation: For a twist, stir in 1/4 cup rum.

rockin' raspberry refresher

(pictured at right)

$\frac{1}{2}$ cup fresh or thawed frozen unsweetened raspberries
$\frac{1}{4}$ cup frozen pink lemonade concentrate
2 cups club soda, chilled

1. Place raspberries and lemonade concentrate in blender. Blend until smooth. Add $\frac{1}{2}$ cup club soda; blend until mixed.

2. Pour remaining $1\frac{1}{2}$ cups club soda into small pitcher. Add raspberry mixture; stir. Pour into glasses; serve immediately.   *Makes 2 servings*

cranberry pear ginger smoothie

2 cups peeled and diced pears *or* 1 can (15 ounces) sliced pears, drained
$1\frac{1}{2}$ cups apple juice
$\frac{1}{2}$ cup whole berry cranberry sauce
$\frac{1}{2}$ teaspoon ground ginger
2 to 3 ice cubes

1. Combine pears and apple juice in blender. Blend until mixture is smooth. Add cranberry sauce and ginger; blend well. Add 2 to 3 ice cubes. Blend until smooth.

2. Pour smoothie into 2 glasses. Serve immediately.

Makes 2 (12-ounce) servings

sparkling strawberry-lime shakes

2 cups (10 ounces) frozen whole unsweetened strawberries
1¼ cups lime-flavored sparkling water, divided
¼ cup whipping cream or half-and-half
1 tablespoon sugar
Lime wedges or slices

1. Place strawberries in blender; let stand 5 minutes to thaw. Add 1 cup sparkling water, cream and sugar. Blend until smooth, scraping down side of blender once or twice (mixture will be thick).

2. Gently stir in remaining ¼ cup sparkling water; pour into 2 glasses. Garnish with lime wedges. *Makes 2 servings*

Variations: **For a tropical variation, add 1 teaspoon banana extract and/or ½ teaspoon coconut extract along with the cream. For a rum-flavored drink add ½ teaspoon rum extract.**

Strawberries are a great choice for melding more than one fruit flavor. Make tasty variations of smoothies by combining one or more of the following ingredients with strawberries: a banana, pineapple chunks, chocolate syrup, peanut butter, protein powder, blueberries, peaches, orange juice, mango cubes or kiwi slices.

triple strawberry smoothie

(pictured at right)

1 cup fresh or frozen strawberries
1 cup milk
3 to 4 tablespoons strawberry jam
1 cup vanilla or strawberry frozen yogurt
1 to 3 ice cubes

1. Combine strawberries, milk and jam in blender. Blend until fruit is puréed and mixture is smooth.

2. Add frozen yogurt and blend until smooth. Add 3 ice cubes if using fresh fruit and 1 to 2 ice cubes if using frozen fruit. Blend until smooth. Pour into 2 glasses. Serve immediately.   *Makes 2 (12-ounce) servings*

Note: Use strawberry milk for extra strawberry flavor.

anti-stress smoothie

2 cups frozen blueberries
1 cup milk
1 cup vanilla frozen yogurt
1 ripe banana
1 tablespoon honey
4 to 6 ice cubes

1. Place blueberries, milk, yogurt, banana, honey and ice cubes in blender. Blend 30 seconds to 1 minute or until mixture is smooth.

2. Pour into 4 glasses. Serve immediately.   *Makes 4 servings*

Note: Lavender is a calming agent. If your supermarket or floral shop has unsprayed sprigs of lavender, remove the flowering buds and sprinkle about $1/2$ teaspoon over each serving. Or, sprinkle with dried lavender.

Citrus
sensations

key lime pie refresher

(pictured on page 105)

1 graham cracker, finely crushed
2 cups ice cubes
1 can (14 ounces) sweetened condensed milk
1 cup half-and-half
1 cup key lime juice
1 tablespoon grated lime peel
   Whipped cream
   Lime slices (optional)

1. Place cracker crumbs in small shallow dish. Wet rims of glasses with damp paper towel; dip rims into crumbs.

2. Place ice cubes, milk, half-and-half, lime juice and lime peel in blender container. Blend about 1 minute or until smooth.

3. Pour into 4 glasses. Garnish with dollop of whipped cream and lime slice. Sprinkle of graham cracker crumbs.   *Makes 4 servings*

dreamsicle smoothie

$1\frac{1}{2}$ cups vanilla yogurt
$\frac{3}{4}$ cup frozen orange juice concentrate
$\frac{1}{2}$ cup milk
$\frac{1}{4}$ teaspoon vanilla
   2 cups ice cubes

1. Combine yogurt, juice concentrate, milk, vanilla and ice in blender. Blend until smooth.

2. Pour into 4 glasses. Serve immediately.   *Makes 4 servings*

citrus punch

4 oranges, sectioned
1 pint strawberries, stemmed and halved
1 to 2 limes, cut into $\frac{1}{8}$-inch slices
1 lemon, cut into $\frac{1}{8}$-inch slices
1 cup raspberries
2 cups orange juice
2 cups grapefruit juice
$\frac{3}{4}$ cup lime juice
$\frac{1}{2}$ cup light corn syrup
1 bottle (750 mL) ginger ale, white grape juice, Asti Spumante or sparkling wine
Fresh mint sprigs (optional)

1. Spread orange sections, strawberries, lime slices, lemon slices and raspberries on baking sheet. Freeze 4 hours or until firm.

2. Combine orange juice, grapefruit juice, lime juice and corn syrup in 2-quart pitcher. Stir until corn syrup dissolves. Refrigerate 2 hours or until cold. Stir in ginger ale just before serving.

3. Divide frozen fruit between 8 (12-ounce) glasses or 10 wide-rimmed wine glasses. Fill glasses with punch. Garnish with mint sprigs. Serve immediately.   *Makes 8 to 10 servings (about 5 cups)*

Citrus Sensations

lemon basil smoothie

2 cups lemon sorbet
1 cup milk
1 container (6 ounces) vanilla yogurt
$\frac{1}{3}$ cup fresh lemon juice
2 tablespoons chopped fresh basil
2 teaspoons finely grated lemon peel
1 cup ice cubes
Fresh basil (optional)
Lemon peel (optional)

1. Place sorbet, milk, yogurt, lemon juice, basil, lemon peel and ice in blender. Blend until smooth, stopping once to scrape down sides.

2. Pour smoothie into 3 glasses. Garnish with basil and lemon peel. Serve immediately.   *Makes 3 servings*

tip

For best storage, fresh basil leaves can be puréed with a small amount of water and put into ice cube trays; the frozen cubes can then be stored in plastic freezer bags and used as needed.

mandarin orange smoothie

(pictured at right)

1 can (11 ounces) mandarin orange sections, drained
1 cup orange sherbet
1 container (6 ounces) orange crème yogurt
$\frac{1}{2}$ cup orange-tangerine juice or orange juice, chilled

1. Combine orange sections, sherbet, yogurt and juice in blender. Blend until nearly smooth.

2. Serve in glasses.   *Makes 2$\frac{1}{4}$ cups or 3 (6-ounce) servings*

peach-lemon frost

3 fresh California peaches, peeled, halved, pitted and quartered
1 cup 2% low-fat milk
$\frac{1}{2}$ cup fresh lemon juice
3 ice cubes, crushed
2 teaspoons grated lemon peel
$\frac{1}{2}$ pint vanilla ice milk

Add peaches to food processor or blender. Process until smooth to measure 2 cups. Add low-fat milk, lemon juice, ice cubes and lemon peel. Process until smooth. Continue processing at low speed; slowly add ice milk until well blended. Pour into glasses. Serve immediately.

Makes 4 servings

Favorite recipe from **California Tree Fruit Agreement**

citrus cooler

(pictured at right)

    2 cups orange juice
    2 cups unsweetened pineapple juice
    1 teaspoon lemon juice
    3/4 teaspoon coconut extract
    3/4 teaspoon vanilla
    2 cups cold sparkling water
      Ice cubes

1. Combine orange juice, pineapple juice, lemon juice, coconut extract and vanilla in large pitcher; refrigerate until cold.

2. To serve, stir in sparkling water. Serve over ice.   *Makes 9 servings*

gingerbread with lemon sauce shake

    3 cups milk
    2 cups French vanilla ice cream
    1/4 cup unsulphered molasses
    1 tablespoon grated lemon peel
    3/4 teaspoon ground ginger
    1/2 teaspoon ground cinnamon
      Whipped cream
    3 lemon wafers, finely crushed

1. Place milk, ice cream, molasses, lemon peel, ginger and cinnamon in blender. Blend about 1 minute or until smooth.

2. Pour shake into 4 glasses. Garnish with dollop of whipped cream and sprinkle of lemon wafer crumbs.   *Makes 4 servings*

cranberry orange smoothie

2 cups fresh or frozen peach slices
1¼ cups orange juice
½ cup whole berry cranberry sauce
1 to 3 ice cubes

1. Combine peaches, orange juice and cranberry sauce in blender. Blend until fruit is puréed and mixture is smooth.

2. Add 3 ice cubes if using fresh fruit and 1 to 2 ice cubes if using frozen fruit. Blend until smooth. Pour smoothie into 2 glasses. Serve immediately.

Makes 2 (12-ounce) servings

The thickness of a smoothie is personal preference. To make smoothies thicker, add more frozen fruit or ice. Yogurt, frozen yogurt and ice cream also make smoothies thicker.

chilled lemon sunset

1½ cups water, divided
½ cup sugar
1 pint lemon sorbet
½ cup orange juice
¼ cup freshly squeezed lemon juice
4 teaspoons grenadine
4 lemon slices

1. Combine ½ cup water and sugar in small saucepan over medium-high heat. Bring to a boil, stirring to dissolve sugar. Boil 1 minute. Transfer mixture to pitcher. Cool to room temperature; chill 1 hour.

2. Combine remaining 1 cup water, sugar syrup, sorbet, orange juice, and lemon juice in blender. Blend until smooth.

3. Pour 1 teaspoon grenadine into bottom of each of 4 glasses. Pour in sorbet mixture. Garnish each with 1 lemon slice. Serve immediately.

Makes 4 servings

To make simple syrup in the microwave, put equal parts sugar and water in a microwavable container or heatproof measuring cup. Microwave on HIGH until the mixture boils and thickens (about 2 to 3 minutes). Stir once until the sugar is completely dissolved. Set aside to cool, then pour into a sterile glass bottle. Store in the refrigerator.

ginger-cucumber limeade

(pictured at right)

1$\frac{1}{2}$ cups chopped, seeded and peeled cucumber
$\frac{1}{3}$ cup frozen limeade concentrate, thawed
1 teaspoon grated fresh ginger
1 cup club soda or sparkling water, chilled
Ice cubes
Thick cucumber slices (optional)
Lime peel (optional)

1. Combine chopped cucumber, limeade and ginger in blender. Blend until nearly smooth.

2. Gently stir together cucumber mixture and club soda in 1-quart pitcher. Serve immediately over ice cubes. Garnish with cucumber slices and lime peel, if desired. *Makes 2$\frac{1}{4}$ cups or 3 (6-ounce) servings*

honey lemonade

Concentrate
6 tablespoons honey
1 cup lemon juice
1 lemon, thinly sliced

Mixer
Ice cubes
1 quart carbonated water

1. For concentrate, dissolve honey in lemon juice in 1-quart jar or glass bowl. Add lemon slices and refrigerate until ready to use.

2. For mixer, fill 12-ounce glass with ice cubes. Add $\frac{1}{4}$ cup lemon juice concentrate and fill glass with carbonated water. *Makes 4 servings*

Tip: Garnish with a lemon wedge.

Favorite recipe from **National Honey Board**

passion potion

(pictured at top right)

1½ cups pink grapefruit juice, chilled
3 tablespoons honey
Ice cubes
¼ cup rum or vodka*

If desired, omit rum or vodka and top each glass with ¼ cup club soda.

Combine grapefruit juice and honey in pitcher; stir until honey is dissolved
Fill two 12-ounce glasses with ice. Pour 2 tablespoons rum over ice in each
glass and add grapefruit juice mixture.   *Makes 2 cups*

Favorite recipe from **National Honey Board**

honey orange marys

(pictured at bottom right)

4 cups tomato juice
½ cup orange juice
¼ cup honey
2 teaspoons prepared horseradish
½ teaspoon celery salt
Hot pepper sauce to taste
Worcestershire sauce to taste
Pepper to taste
Ice cubes
Celery sticks (optional)

Combine tomato juice, orange juice, honey, horseradish and celery salt in
large pitcher; stir until well blended. Season to taste with hot pepper sauce,
Worcestershire sauce and black pepper. Serve over ice in tall glasses.
Garnish with celery sticks, if desired.   *Makes about 5 cups*

Favorite recipe from **National Honey Board**

strawberry limeade

1½ cups quartered fresh strawberries
1 cup lime juice
4 cups water
1½ cups EQUAL® SPOONFUL*
6 small whole strawberries or lime wedges (optional)

*May substitute 36 packets EQUAL® sweetener.

• Blend strawberries and lime juice in blender or food processor until smooth. Combine strawberry mixture, water and Equal® in pitcher.

• Pour over ice cubes in tall glasses; garnish each with strawberry or lime wedge, if desired. *Makes 6 servings*

Fruit drinks with fresh fruit and juices—the perfect cooldown after a hot, sticky summer day—are healthy alternatives to soft drinks. They tend to be low-fat, high in vitamins A and C, and a rich source of cancer-fighting antioxidants.

lemon chiffon cooler

2 cups milk
1 pint lemon sorbet, softened
1 cup French vanilla ice cream, softened
$\frac{1}{3}$ cup strained lemon juice
2 teaspoons grated lemon peel, plus extra for garnish
1 tablespoon sugar
Whipped cream

1. Place milk, sorbet, ice cream, lemon juice, lemon peel and sugar in blender. Blend until smooth.

2. Pour cooler into 4 glasses. Top each glass with dollop of whipped cream and sprinkle of lemon peel. Serve immediately. *Makes 4 servings*

tip

When grating lemon peel, be sure to use only the yellow part of the peel and not the bitter white part. Grate the peel before you juice the lemon.

tofu orange dream

(pictured at right)

½ cup soft tofu
½ cup orange juice
1 container (about 2½ ounces) baby food carrots
2 tablespoons honey *or* 1 tablespoon sugar
¼ teaspoon fresh grated ginger
2 to 3 ice cubes

1. Place all ingredients in blender. Blend 15 seconds or until smooth.

2. Pour into glass; serve immediately. *Makes 1 (1-cup) serving*

pineapple-mint lemonade

1 cup sugar
⅔ cup water
⅓ cup chopped fresh mint
1 can (46 ounces) DOLE® Pineapple Juice
1 cup lemon juice
Fresh mint sprigs (optional)

• Combine sugar and water in large saucepan; bring to boil. Boil 1 minute; remove from heat.

• Stir in chopped mint; let stand 15 minutes.

• Strain liquid into punch bowl; discard chopped mint. Add pineapple and lemon juice. Serve over ice cubes in tall glasses. Garnish with mint sprigs, if desired. *Makes 8 servings*

Summer Spritzer: **Combine 2 cups Pineapple-Mint Lemonade with 2 cups mineral or sparkling water. Serve over ice. Makes 4 servings.**

Prep Time: **15 minutes**
Cook/Stand Time: **20 minutes**

mandarin orange, coconut and lime cooler

(pictured at right)

1 can (15 ounces) mandarin oranges in light syrup, undrained
2 tablespoons corn syrup
1 tablespoon lime juice
1 teaspoon grated lime peel
1 teaspoon grated fresh ginger
1 teaspoon coconut extract
$\frac{1}{2}$ teaspoon orange extract
1 cup ice cubes
Basil or mint leaves (optional)
Lime slices (optional)

1. Place oranges with juice, corn syrup, lime juice, lime peel, ginger, coconut extract, orange extract and ice cubes in blender. Blend about 10 seconds or until ice is crushed.

2. Pour into 2 serving glasses. Garnish with basil leaves and lime slices. Serve immediately. *Makes 3 servings*

real old-fashioned lemonade

Juice of 6 SUNKIST® lemons (1 cup)
$\frac{3}{4}$ cup sugar, or to taste
4 cups cold water
1 SUNKIST® lemon, cut into cartwheel slices
Ice cubes

In large pitcher, combine lemon juice and sugar; stir to dissolve sugar. Add remaining ingredients; blend well. *Makes about 6 cups*

Pink Lemonade: Add a few drops of red food coloring or grenadine syrup.

Honeyed Lemonade: Substitute honey to taste for the sugar.

festive citrus punch

1 can (6 ounces) frozen Florida grapefruit juice concentrate, thawed
1 can (6 ounces) frozen pineapple juice concentrate, thawed
1 cup water
3 tablespoons honey
2 tablespoons grenadine syrup (optional)
1 bottle (1 liter) ginger ale, chilled
  Mint sprigs for garnish (optional)
  Ice cubes

Combine grapefruit juice, pineapple juice, water and honey in punch bowl or large pitcher. Stir in grenadine, if desired. Stir until well combined.

Just before serving, slowly pour ginger ale down side of punch bowl. Stir gently to combine. Garnish, if desired. Serve over ice in chilled glasses.

Makes about 18 (4-ounce) servings

Favorite recipe from **Florida Department of Citrus**

tip

Transform coolers and punches into party drinks with fancy ice cubes. To make fun-shaped cubes, freeze water or juice in star or letter-shaped ice cube trays. To make decorative fruit-filled cubes, freeze herbs or fruit in regular ice cube trays. First, fill the trays halfway with water, add the food and freeze until set. Then add more water to fill the trays and freeze again.

Fruity
favorites

peachy keen smoothie

(pictured on page 133)

    1 package (16 ounces) frozen peaches *or* 2 cups peeled and sliced
       fresh peaches
1$\frac{1}{2}$ cups orange sherbet
    1 can (11$\frac{1}{2}$ ounces) peach nectar
    1 banana
    1 cup ice
    Fresh mint (optional)

1. Place peaches, sherbet, nectar, banana and ice in blender. Blend until smooth, stopping once to scrape down sides.

2. Pour smoothie into 4 glasses. Garnish with mint. Serve immediately.

Makes 4 servings

grape roughie

$\frac{1}{2}$ cup Chilean seedless green grapes
$\frac{1}{2}$ cup 1% milk
$\frac{1}{2}$ cup plain low-fat yogurt
 1 tablespoon brown sugar
$\frac{1}{8}$ teaspoon vanilla
 2 ice cubes, cracked

Place all ingredients in blender. Blend at high speed 15 seconds or until smooth. Serve immediately.
Makes 1$\frac{1}{2}$ cups (1 serving)

Favorite recipe from **Chilean Fresh Fruit Association**

red hot apple mugs

4 teaspoons red cinnamon candies
1 quart apple juice
1/2 teaspoon cinnamon or peppermint extract (optional)
4 candy cinnamon or peppermint sticks (5 inches each)

1. Place 1 teaspoon cinnamon candies in each of 4 mugs. Heat apple juice and cinnamon extract, if desired, in medium saucepan over medium heat until hot; do not boil.

2. Pour hot juice into mugs; add cinnamon stick for stirring.

Makes 4 servings

Note: Candies will completely dissolve into apple juice and color the juice red after about 10 minutes.

Prep Time: 5 minutes

Increase the number of servings of fruit in your daily diet with 100% apple juice. Create new and delicious hot and cold beverages by combining apple juice with other juices or by adding herbs and spices.

guava fruit punch

(pictured at right)

1½ cups boiling water
2 decaffeinated tea bags
3 thin slices peeled fresh ginger (about 1 inch in diameter)
2 cups guava juice
¾ cup pineapple juice
1 to 2 tablespoons lemon juice
Ice cubes

1. Combine water, tea bags and ginger in heatproof pitcher; steep 5 minutes. Discard tea bags and ginger. Cool to room temperature.

2. Add guava juice, pineapple juice and lemon juice to tea mixture; mix well. Serve in tall glasses over ice.   *Makes 4 servings*

sparkling ginger-apple cider

Ice cubes
¾ cup apple juice
¾ cup ginger ale
⅛ teaspoon vanilla

Place 3 ice cubes in tall glass. Pour apple juice, ginger ale and vanilla over ice; stir until combined.   *Makes 1 (12-ounce) serving*

Sparkling Ginger-Apple Float: **Prepare as directed, omitting ice cubes. Float scoop of vanilla ice cream on top.**

spiced passion fruit-yogurt starter

(pictured at right)

1 cup plain yogurt
1 ripe banana, cut into pieces
1 cup sliced fresh strawberries
$1/4$ cup frozen passion fruit juice concentrate or frozen apple-passion-mango fruit juice concentrate, thawed
$3/4$ teaspoon pumpkin pie spice
$1/8$ teaspoon ground white pepper

1. Combine yogurt, banana, strawberries, juice concentrate, pumpkin pie spice and white pepper in blender. Blend until nearly smooth.

2. Pour into glasses. Serve immediately.

Makes $2^1/3$ cups or about 3 (6-ounce) servings

plum purple frappé

3 fresh California plums, halved, pitted and coarsely chopped
$1/2$ cup plain low-fat yogurt
2 tablespoons wheat germ
2 tablespoons honey
3 ice cubes, cracked

Add plums, yogurt, wheat germ, honey and ice cubes to food processor or blender. Process until smooth. Serve immediately.   *Makes 2 servings*

Favorite recipe from **California Tree Fruit Agreement**

banana-pineapple breakfast shake

2 cups plain yogurt
1 can (8 ounces) crushed pineapple in juice, undrained
1 ripe banana
3 tablespoons sugar
1 teaspoon vanilla
$\frac{1}{8}$ teaspoon ground nutmeg
1 cup ice cubes

1. Place yogurt, pineapple, banana, sugar, vanilla, nutmeg and ice in blender. Blend until smooth.

2. Pour into 4 serving glasses.

Makes 4 servings

Tip: This recipe is perfect for a brunch party or another special occasion. Make as many batches as you need to serve everyone.

Prep Time: 5 minutes

frozen rainbow bubblers

1 packet (2-quart size) fruit flavored powdered drink mix
2 cups water
1 bottle (2 liters) ginger ale, chilled

1. Dissolve powdered drink mix in water, stirring to mix well. Pour into 1½ ice cube trays (should make about 16 ice cubes). Freeze until solid.

2. Place 3 ice cubes in glass. Fill glass with ginger ale; stir gently.

Makes 5 servings

For an extra layer of flavor, prepare ice cubes from 2 or more of your favorite flavors of drink mix or fruit juices. Keep ice cubes sealed in airtight containers or freezer bags until ready to use.

striped grape smoothie

   5 red seedless grapes
   ¼ cup grape jelly
   2 scoops vanilla ice cream or frozen yogurt
   ¾ cup milk

1. Wrap grapes in plastic wrap. Freeze grapes and 1 clear serving glass at least 30 minutes or until very cold.

2. Place grape jelly in microwavable bowl. Microwave on HIGH 15 seconds or until melted. Cool until mixture has consistency of thick syrup.

3. Remove serving glass from freezer. Using the tip of a small spoon, drip small amount of jelly syrup inside rim of glass to form "stripes." Place glass back in freezer until needed.

4. Place ice cream, milk and remaining jelly syrup in blender. Blend 10 seconds or until smooth. Pour smoothie into prepared glass. Top with frozen grapes. Serve immediately.   *Makes 1 serving*

Note: When serving this delicious smoothie to small children, omit the frozen grapes.

tofu, fruit & veggie smoothies

(pictured at right)

1 cup frozen pineapple chunks
$\frac{1}{2}$ cup soft tofu
$\frac{1}{2}$ cup apple juice
$\frac{1}{2}$ cup orange juice
1 container (about $2\frac{1}{2}$ ounces) baby food carrots

1. Place all ingredients in blender. Blend 15 to 30 seconds until smooth, using on/off pulsing action to break up chunks.

2. Pour into glasses; serve immediately.   *Makes 2 (1-cup) servings*

peach smoothie

2 cups frozen sliced peaches
1 container (6 ounces) peach yogurt
$\frac{1}{2}$ cup milk
$\frac{1}{4}$ teaspoon vanilla

1. Combine peaches, yogurt, milk and vanilla in blender. Blend until smooth.

2. Pour into glasses. Serve immediately.   *Makes 2 servings*

Prep Time: **5 minutes**

carrot cake smoothie

(pictured at right and on back cover)

4 jars (4 ounces each) baby food carrots
1 cup vanilla frozen yogurt
$\frac{1}{2}$ cup milk
$\frac{1}{4}$ cup sugar
$\frac{1}{2}$ teaspoon ground cinnamon
$\frac{1}{8}$ teaspoon ground ginger
   Dash ground nutmeg
   Dash salt
2 ice cubes
4 carrots (optional)

1. Place carrots, frozen yogurt, milk, sugar, cinnamon, ginger, nutmeg, salt and ice cubes in blender. Blend 30 seconds to 1 minute or until mixture is frothy and ice cubes are finely ground.

2. Pour into 4 glasses. Garnish each with carrot for stirring. Serve immediately. *Makes 4 servings*

apricot peachy chillers

1 can (about 9 ounces) apricots in heavy syrup
1 cup cut-up frozen peach slices
$\frac{1}{2}$ cup frozen whole unsweetened strawberries
1 container (6 ounces) vanilla yogurt
1 to 2 tablespoons lemon juice (optional)

1. Place all ingredients in blender. Blend 15 to 30 seconds or until smooth, using on/off pulsing action to break up chunks.

2. Divide between 4 glasses; serve immediately.

Makes 4 ($\frac{3}{4}$-cup) servings

Soy Apricot Peachy Chiller: **Substitute 1 container (6 ounces) vanilla or peach soy yogurt for the regular vanilla yogurt.**

frozen watermelon whip

(pictured at right)

1³/₄ cups ice
  1 cup coarsely chopped seedless watermelon
  1 cup brewed lemon-flavored herbal tea, at room temperature
  Lime slices (optional)

1. Combine all ingredients in blender. Blend until smooth, pulsing as necessary to break up all ice.

2. Pour into 2 tall glasses; garnish with lime. Serve immediately.

Makes 2 servings

soy milk smoothie

3 cups plain or vanilla soy milk
1 banana, peeled and frozen (see Tip)
1 cup frozen strawberries or raspberries
1 teaspoon vanilla or almond extract
¹/₃ cup EQUAL® SPOONFUL*

*May substitute 8 packets EQUAL® sweetener.

• Place all ingredients in blender or food processor. Blend until smooth.

Makes 4 servings

Tip: Peel and cut banana into large chunks. Place in plastic freezer bag, seal and freeze at least 5 to 6 hours or overnight.

banana-coconut "cream pie" smoothie

3 ripe bananas

$1\frac{1}{2}$ cups unsweetened canned coconut milk, chilled (do not use coconut cream)

$1\frac{1}{2}$ cups pineapple juice, chilled

2 tablespoons sugar

$\frac{1}{2}$ teaspoon vanilla

$\frac{1}{8}$ teaspoon ground nutmeg

3 ice cubes

Toasted shredded sweetened coconut (optional)

1. Peel bananas and break into chunks. Place in blender. Add coconut milk, pineapple juice, sugar, vanilla, nutmeg and ice cubes.

2. Blend about 30 seconds to 1 minute or until mixture is frothy and ice cubes are finely ground. Pour into 4 glasses. Garnish with toasted coconut.

Makes 4 servings

Note: If desired, combine the ingredients in a large pitcher and purée using an immersion blender.

pineapple-lemonade pizzazz

3 cups peach nectar, mango nectar, peach-mango juice or passion
    fruit juice, chilled
3 cups pineapple juice, chilled
1 can (12 ounces) frozen lemonade concentrate, thawed
2 cups (about 16 ounces) ginger ale, chilled
2½ cups club soda or sparkling water, chilled
    Crushed ice

1. Combine peach nectar, pineapple juice and lemonade concentrate
in 1-gallon pitcher.

2. Gently stir in ginger ale and club soda. Serve immediately over
crushed ice. *Makes 12 cups or 16 (6-ounce) servings*

Many drink combinations are easy to prepare ahead of time
to have on hand for any occasion. Follow the recipe directions
and store in the refrigerator for up to one week. Always add the
carbonated beverages or soda just before serving.

banana smoothie

1 packet CREAM OF WHEAT® Maple Brown Sugar Instant Hot Cereal,
   uncooked
$\frac{2}{3}$ cup boiling water
1 large banana
1 cup ice cubes
1 teaspoon honey or MAPLE GROVE FARMS® of Vermont Pure Maple
   Syrup

Place Cream of Wheat and boiling water in blender container; cover. Blend
on low speed 1 minute. Add banana; blend 30 seconds longer. Add ice and
honey; cover. Blend on high speed until smooth. Serve immediately.

Makes 2 servings

Tip: Use CREAM OF WHEAT® Apples 'n Cinnamon, Strawberries 'n Cream or
Cinnamon Swirl Instant Hot Cereal to create new delicious flavors.

Prep Time: **5 minutes**
Total Time: **10 minutes**

frozen apple slushies

(pictured at right)

1 cup 100% cranberry juice, chilled
$\frac{1}{2}$ cup frozen unsweetened apple juice concentrate, thawed
1 large Red Delicious apple, peeled and cut into chunks
$\frac{1}{8}$ teaspoon ground cinnamon
3 cups ice cubes

1. Place cranberry juice, apple juice concentrate, apple chunks and cinnamon in blender. Blend until smooth. Add ice cubes; blend using on/off pulsing action until smooth and icy.

2. Pour into 4 glasses. Serve immediately.   *Makes 4 servings*

Note: Freeze any leftovers in 1-cup servings in small airtight microwavable containers. To serve, microwave each serving for 15 seconds on HIGH; stir. Continue microwaving in 10-second increments until slushy.

cantaloupe smoothie

(pictured on front cover)

3 cups seeded, peeled and cubed cantaloupe
2 containers (6 ounces each) orange crème yogurt
$\frac{1}{2}$ cup orange-tangerine juice or orange juice, chilled
1 tablespoon honey
1 teaspoon vanilla
4 small cantaloupe wedges (optional)

1. Combine cubed cantaloupe, yogurt, juice, honey and vanilla in blender. Blend until nearly smooth.

2. Pour into glasses. Garnish with cantaloupe wedges. Serve immediately.
Makes $3\frac{1}{2}$ cups or about 4 (6-ounce) servings

ginger-pineapple spritzer

(pictured at right)

2 cups pineapple juice or cranberry juice
1 tablespoon chopped crystallized ginger
1 cup chilled club soda or sparkling water
  Ice cubes
  Fresh pineapple wedges (optional)

1. Combine pineapple juice and ginger in small saucepan. Bring to a simmer. Pour into small bowl. Cover; refrigerate 8 to 24 hours.

2. Strain juice mixture; discard ginger. Gently stir club soda into juice. Serve in glasses over ice cubes. Garnish with pineapple wedges.

Makes 3 cups or 4 (6-ounce) servings

tofu peanut butter smoothie

1 banana, cut into chunks
$\frac{1}{2}$ cup soft tofu
$\frac{1}{4}$ cup creamy peanut butter
2 tablespoons honey *or* 1 tablespoon sugar
1 teaspoon vanilla
1 to 2 ice cubes

1. Place all ingredients in blender. Blend 15 to 30 seconds or until smooth, using on/off pulsing action to break up ice.

2. Pour into glass; serve immediately.

Makes 1 (1-cup) serving

vermont maple smoothie

1½ cups unsweetened applesauce
1 cup vanilla frozen yogurt
1 cup milk
3 tablespoons maple syrup
½ teaspoon ground cinnamon
2 ice cubes
Ground nutmeg

1. Combine applesauce, frozen yogurt, milk, maple syrup, cinnamon and ice cubes in blender. Blend about 30 seconds to 1 minute or until mixture is frothy and ice cubes are finely ground.

2. Pour into 4 glasses. Sprinkle with nutmeg.   *Makes 4 servings*

Note: This smoothie can be made several hours in advance and chilled. Mix well before serving. It will not be as frothy.

wow watermelon smoothie

(pictured at right)

4$\frac{1}{2}$ cups cubed seedless watermelon
1$\frac{1}{2}$ cups strawberry sorbet
1$\frac{1}{2}$ cups cubed or crushed ice
  1 banana

1. Place watermelon, sorbet, ice and banana in blender. Blend until smooth, stopping once to scrape down sides.

2. Divide smoothie between 4 sugar-rimmed* glasses.

Makes 4 servings

*See page 86.

sparkling apple punch

  2 bottles (750 mL each) sparkling apple cider, chilled
1$\frac{1}{2}$ quarts papaya or apricot nectar, chilled
    Ice cubes
  1 or 2 papayas, peeled and chopped
    Orange slices, quartered

Combine apple cider, papaya nectar and ice in punch bowl. Add papaya and orange slices.

Makes about 4 quarts

quick apple punch

(pictured at right)

4 cups MOTT'S® Apple Juice
2 cups cranberry juice cocktail
2 tablespoons lemon juice
1 liter ginger ale, chilled
   Crushed ice, as needed

In large bowl, combine apple juice, cranberry juice and lemon juice. Fifteen minutes before serving, add ginger ale and crushed ice. Do not stir.

Makes 15 servings

raspberry watermelon slush

1 cup frozen raspberries
1 cup watermelon cubes, seeded
1 cup lemon-lime seltzer
1 tablespoon sugar

Combine all ingredients in blender or food processor. Blend thoroughly. Serve immediately.

Makes 2 servings

Favorite recipe from **The Sugar Association, Inc.**

strawberry delights

(pictured at right)

2 cups strawberry ice cream
1 cup sliced fresh strawberries
$2/3$ cup milk
$1/4$ cup cold orange juice
$1/8$ teaspoon ground cinnamon
   Additional fresh fruit (optional)
   Mint sprigs (optional)

1. Place ice cream, strawberries, milk, orange juice and cinnamon in blender. Blend until smooth.

2. Pour into glasses. Garnish with additional fruit and mint sprigs.

Makes 4 servings

fruit 'n juice breakfast shake

1 extra-ripe, medium DOLE® Banana
$3/4$ cup DOLE® Pineapple Juice
$1/2$ cup lowfat vanilla yogurt
$1/2$ cup DOLE® Frozen Blueberries

Combine all ingredients in blender. Process until smooth.

Makes 2 servings

frozen florida monkey malts

(pictured at right)

2 bananas, peeled
1 cup milk
5 tablespoons frozen orange juice concentrate
3 tablespoons malted milk powder

1. Wrap bananas in plastic wrap; freeze.

2. Break bananas into pieces; place in blender with milk, orange juice concentrate and malted milk powder. Blend until smooth; pour into glasses to serve. *Makes 2 servings*

apple pie shake

1 (14-ounce) can EAGLE BRAND® Sweetened Condensed Milk (NOT evaporated milk), chilled
1 cup applesauce, chilled
$\frac{1}{2}$ cup apple juice or apple cider, chilled
$\frac{1}{2}$ teaspoon apple pie spice*
3 cups crushed ice
Apple wedges and apple peel strips (optional)

Look for apple pie spice in the spice section of your supermarket, or substitute a mixture of $\frac{1}{4}$ teaspoon ground cinnamon, $\frac{1}{8}$ teaspoon ground nutmeg and a dash of ground allspice.

1. In blender, combine EAGLE BRAND®, applesauce, apple juice and apple pie spice; cover and blend until smooth.

2. With blender running, gradually add ice, blending until smooth. Serve immediately. Garnish with apple wedges and apple peel strips (optional).
Makes 4 or 5 servings

Prep Time: **5 minutes**

Tropical
treasures

cuban guava punch

(pictured on page 173)

 2 cups water
³/₄ cup sugar
1¹/₂ cups guava nectar or ruby red grapefruit juice drink,* chilled
1¹/₂ cups orange juice, chilled
 ¹/₂ cup pineapple juice, chilled
 ¹/₄ cup freshly squeezed lime juice*
   Ice cubes
   Fresh pineapple wedges (optional)

If using a ruby red grapefruit juice drink, reduce lime juice to 2 tablespoons.

1. Combine water and sugar in small saucepan. Cook and stir over medium heat until sugar dissolves. Cool to room temperature.

2. Combine sugar mixture, guava nectar, orange juice, pineapple juice and lime juice; mix well. Serve over ice cubes. Garnish with fresh pineapple wedge.   *Makes 6¹/₄ cups or about 8 servings*

island delight smoothie

2 cups chopped fresh or jarred mango
1 container (16 ounces) plain yogurt
1$\frac{1}{2}$ cups pineapple-orange juice, chilled
1$\frac{1}{2}$ cups ice
1 cup chopped pineapple
1 banana, peeled, quartered and frozen
$\frac{1}{2}$ cup sliced fresh strawberries
2 tablespoons honey
Pineapple wedge (optional)

1. Place mango, yogurt, juice, ice, pineapple, banana, strawberries and honey in blender. Blend until smooth.

2. Divide smoothie between 4 glasses. Garnish with pineapple wedge. Serve immediately. *Makes 4 servings*

sangrita

3 cups DEL MONTE® Tomato Juice
1$\frac{1}{2}$ cups orange juice
$\frac{1}{2}$ cup salsa
Juice of 1 medium lime

1. Mix all ingredients in large pitcher; chill.

2. Serve over ice with fruit garnishes, if desired.

Makes 6 (6-ounce) servings

Prep Time: 3 minutes

sparkling pomegranate gingerade

$\frac{1}{2}$ cup sugar

$\frac{1}{4}$ cup water

1 teaspoon grated lemon peel

1 thin slice fresh ginger (about 1 inch in diameter)

2 cups seltzer water

2 cups pomegranate juice

Ice cubes

Mint leaves (optional)

1. Combine sugar, water, lemon peel and ginger in small saucepan. Bring mixture to a boil over medium heat. Boil 1 minute. Set aside to cool.

2. Strain cooled syrup into large pitcher; discard solids. Stir in seltzer water and pomegranate juice. Pour mixture over ice in 4 serving glasses. Garnish with mint.

Makes 4 servings

hot tropics sipper

4 cups pineapple juice
2 cups apple juice
1 container (about 11 ounces) apricot nectar (1$\frac{1}{3}$ cups)
$\frac{1}{2}$ cup packed dark brown sugar
1 medium lemon, thinly sliced
1 medium orange, thinly sliced
6 whole cloves
3 whole cinnamon sticks
Additional orange and lemon slices (optional)

Slow Cooker Directions

1. Place juices, nectar, lemon, orange, cloves and cinnamon in slow cooker. Cover; cook on HIGH 3$\frac{1}{2}$ to 4 hours or until very fragrant.

2. Strain immediately (beverage will turn bitter if fruit and spices remain after cooking is complete). Garnish with fresh slices of orange and lemon.

Makes 8 servings

Prep Time: **5 minutes**
Cook Time: **3$\frac{1}{2}$ to 4 hours (HIGH)**

lemon-lime watermelon agua fresca

(pictured at right)

  10 cups seedless watermelon cubes
   1 cup ice water
  1/3 cup sugar
   2 tablespoons freshly squeezed lemon juice
   2 tablespoons freshly squeezed lime juice
     Ice cubes

1. Combine half of watermelon and water in blender. Blend until smooth. Transfer to bowl. Repeat with remaining watermelon and water.

2. Add sugar, lemon and lime juices; stir until dissolved. Serve immediately over ice or refrigerate until ready to serve. *Makes 6 servings*

horchata shake

   2 cups rice milk or milk
   1 cup well-cooked rice (see Note)
   1 cup vanilla frozen rice milk ice cream
  1/4 cup sugar
  1/2 teaspoon cinnamon
  1/2 teaspoon vanilla
  1/4 teaspoon salt
   4 ice cubes

1. Combine rice milk, rice, ice cream, sugar, cinnamon, vanilla, salt and ice cubes in blender. Blend 30 seconds to 1 minute or until mixture is frothy and ice cubes are finely ground.

2. Place strainer over pitcher. Pour horchata through strainer. Discard solids. Serve immediately or chill for several hours. Stir well before serving.
Makes 4 servings

Note: Rice should be soft enough to mash with a fork.

sippable gazpacho

2 small celery stalks
2 green onions, trimmed
4 cucumber slices
  Ice cubes
3 cups vegetable juice
1 tablespoon lemon juice
1 tablespoon red wine vinegar
1 teaspoon Worcestershire sauce
3 to 4 drops hot pepper sauce
$\frac{1}{2}$ teaspoon ground cumin
$\frac{1}{8}$ teaspoon black pepper

1. Place 1 celery stalk and 1 green onion in each of 2 glasses. Cut halfway into center of each cucumber slice; place on 2 slices rim of each glass. Fill each glass with ice; set aside.

2. Stir together vegetable juice, lemon juice, vinegar, Worcestershire sauce, pepper sauce, cumin and pepper in pitcher. Pour into prepared glasses. Serve immediately.   *Makes 2 servings*

sparkling tropical fruit combo

(pictured at right)

$^3/_4$ cup orange-tangerine juice or orange juice, chilled
$^3/_4$ cup passion fruit juice or guava-pineapple juice, chilled
$^3/_4$ cup club soda or sparkling water, chilled
    Ice cubes
    Maraschino cherries (optional)

1. Combine orange-tangerine juice and passion fruit juice in 1-quart pitcher. Gently stir in club soda.

2. Serve in glasses over ice cubes. Garnish with maraschino cherries.

Makes 2$^1/_4$ cups or 3 servings

toasted coco colada

    3 ounces MR & MRS T® Piña Colada Mix
1$^1/_2$ ounces coconut rum
  $^1/_2$ ounce caramel syrup
  $^1/_2$ ounce coconut syrup
    1 cup ice
    1 lime wedge
    Toasted coconut flakes, ground (as needed)

Blend first 5 ingredients in blender until slushy. Coat rim of daiquiri glass with lime wedge; dip glass into ground toasted coconut flakes. Pour colada into daiquiri glass.

Makes 1 drink

mango smoothie

1$\frac{1}{2}$ cups chopped mango (fresh, jarred or frozen)
  1 cup guava or mango nectar, chilled
$\frac{2}{3}$ cup (5-ounce can) NESTLÉ® CARNATION® Evaporated Milk
    Juice from 2 limes
  1 tablespoon packed brown sugar
    Ice cubes (optional)
    Sliced almonds (optional)

COMBINE mango, nectar, evaporated milk, lime juice and sugar in blender; cover. Blend until smooth. Serve over ice and top with almonds, if desired.

Makes 2 servings

Prep Time: 5 minutes

melon cooler

3 cups cubed DOLE® Cantaloupe
5 cups DOLE® Pineapple Orange Juice, divided

• Place melon and 1 cup juice in blender or food processor container. Blend until smooth.

• Combine melon mixture and remaining juice in large pitcher. Chill 1 hour before serving. Stir before serving. Garnish with skewered fresh fruit, if desired.

Makes 7 servings

Prep Time: 10 minutes
Chill Time: 1 hour

white sangria

1 carton (64 ounces) DOLE® Pineapple Orange Banana Juice
2 cups fruity white wine
2 cups sliced DOLE® Fresh Strawberries
1 orange, thinly sliced
1 lime, thinly sliced
¼ cup sugar
¼ cup orange-flavored liqueur
Ice cubes
Mint sprigs for garnish

• Combine juice, wine, strawberries, orange, lime, sugar and liqueur in 2 large pitchers; cover and refrigerate 2 hours to blend flavors. Serve over ice. Garnish with mint sprigs.   *Makes 20 servings*

jungle juice

(pictured at right)

1 banana
1 cup frozen strawberries
1 container (6 ounces) vanilla yogurt
2 tablespoons frozen orange juice concentrate
2 tablespoons strawberry syrup
   Fresh orange slices (optional)

1. Place banana, strawberries, yogurt and frozen orange juice concentrate in blender. Blend until smooth, scraping down sides as needed.

2. Evenly drizzle syrup around inside of 2 tall clear glasses. Pour juice mixture into glasses. Garnish with orange slices.   *Makes 2 servings*

mango-ginger smoothie

2 cups cubed fresh or jarred mango
1 bag (16 ounces) frozen sliced peaches *or* 2$\frac{1}{2}$ cups fresh peeled and
   sliced peaches
1 container (6 ounces) vanilla yogurt
2 tablespoons honey
2 teaspoons grated fresh ginger
1 cup ice

1. Place all ingredients in blender container. Blend until smooth, stopping once to scrape down sides.

2. Pour smoothie into 4 glasses. Serve immediately.   *Makes 4 servings*

lemon sangrita punch

1 bottle (64 fluid ounces) V8® 100% Vegetable Juice, chilled
1 container (64 fluid ounces) refrigerated lemonade
1 tablespoon Worcestershire sauce (optional)
2 lemons, thinly sliced
2 limes, thinly sliced
1 orange, thinly sliced

1. Stir the juice, lemonade and Worcestershire, if desired, lemons, limes and orange in an 8-quart punch bowl.

2. Serve immediately or refrigerate until serving time.

3. Pour over ice-filled tall glasses.   *Makes 20 servings*

Prep Time: **10 minutes**

Traditional sangrita is a Spanish drink that is different from sangria. Sangrita is made with tomatoes, citrus juices and chili powder or hot pepper sauce. It is often served with a shot of tequila. This refreshing nonalcoholic version is perfect for a summer party or a morning eye-opener.

pineapple agua fresca

(pictured at right)

3 cups cubed fresh pineapple (about $\frac{1}{2}$ of large pineapple)
$\frac{1}{3}$ cup sugar
$\frac{1}{4}$ cup freshly squeezed lime juice
2 tablespoons minced fresh mint
2 cups club soda, chilled
　Ice cubes
6 mint sprigs

1. Place pineapple, sugar, lime juice and minced mint in blender. Blend about 30 seconds to 1 minute or until mixture is frothy.

2. Pour into pitcher. Stir in club soda. Immediately pour into 6 sugar-dipped* ice-filled glasses. Garnish with mint sprigs.　　　*Makes 6 servings*

*See page 86.

strawberry banana coconut smoothie

2 cups fresh or frozen strawberries
$1\frac{1}{4}$ cups unsweetened canned coconut milk
1 teaspoon rum extract (optional)
1 banana, peeled and sliced
1 to 3 ice cubes

1. Combine strawberries, coconut milk and rum extract, if desired, in blender. Blend until fruit is puréed and mixture is smooth.

2. Add banana; blend. Add 3 ice cubes if using fresh fruit and 1 to 2 ice cubes if using frozen fruit. Blend until smooth. Pour smoothie into 2 glasses. Serve immediately.　　　*Makes 2 to 4 servings*

cuban batido

1½ cups cubed fresh pineapple
1 cup ice cubes
¾ cup milk
½ cup orange juice
3 tablespoons sugar
1 tablespoon freshly squeezed lime juice
Lime slices (optional)

1. Combine pineapple, ice, milk, orange juice, sugar and lime juice in blender. Blend until smooth

2. Pour mixture into 2 tall glasses. Garnish with lime slices.

Makes 2 servings

Tip: A batido is a popular Latin American drink made with water, milk, fruit and ice. It is similar in texture to a smoothie and literally means "beaten" in Portuguese.

tropical breeze smoothies

(pictured at right)

1 cup frozen pineapple chunks
1 cup frozen mango chunks
$\frac{1}{2}$ cup unsweetened canned coconut milk
$\frac{1}{2}$ cup milk
2 tablespoons honey

1. Place all ingredients in blender. Blend 15 to 30 seconds or until smooth, using on/off pulsing action to break up chunks.

2. Divide smoothie between 2 glasses; serve immediately.

Makes 2 servings

sangrita

1 can (12 ounces) tomato juice
$1\frac{1}{2}$ cups orange juice
$\frac{1}{4}$ cup freshly squeezed lime or lemon juice
1 tablespoon finely minced onion
$\frac{1}{4}$ teaspoon hot pepper sauce
$\frac{1}{8}$ teaspoon salt
Ice cubes
4 small stalks celery with leafy tops

1. Combine juices, onion, pepper sauce and salt in 1-quart container with tight-fitting lid. Cover; refrigerate 2 hours or until flavors are blended.

2. Pour into ice-filled glasses. Add celery stalk to each glass for stirrer.

Makes 4 servings

Party
potions

strawberry-mango daiquiri punch

(pictured on page 199)

3 cups cubed fresh mango
3 cups frozen unsweetened whole strawberries
$^3/_4$ cup frozen limeade concentrate, thawed
$^3/_4$ cup light rum or pineapple juice
2$^1/_2$ cups lemon-lime soda
    Ice cubes
    Fresh strawberries (optional)

1. Working in batches, combine mango, strawberries, limeade and rum in blender. Blend until nearly smooth. Pour into 2$^1/_2$-quart pitcher.

2. Gently stir in soda. Serve over ice cubes. Garnish with fresh strawberries.
Makes 7 cups or about 9 servings

kahlúa® parisian coffee

1 ounce cognac or brandy
$^1/_2$ ounce KAHLÚA® Liqueur
$^1/_2$ ounce Grand Marnier
    Hot coffee
    Whipped cream
    Orange peel (optional)

Pour cognac, Kahlúa® and Grand Marnier into steaming cup of coffee. Top with whipped cream. Garnish with orange peel. *Makes 1 serving*

bavarian wild berry cosmopolitan

1 cup boiling water
3 LIPTON® Bavarian Wild Berry Pyramid Tea Bags
2 tablespoons sugar
2 tablespoons pomegranate juice
2 tablespoons vodka
1 tablespoon lime juice
1 tablespoon orange liqueur

Pour boiling water over LIPTON® Bavarian Wild Berry Pyramid Tea Bags; cover and brew 5 minutes. Remove Tea Bags and squeeze, then stir in sugar; chill.

In shaker filled with ice, combine tea with remaining ingredients. Shake well, then strain into chilled martini glasses. Garnish, if desired, with orange or lime curl and blackberries. *Makes 2 servings*

Substitution: For a non-alcohol version, simply omit vodka and orange liquor and add 3 tablespoons orange juice.

Prep Time: 15 minutes
Brew Time: 5 minutes
Chill Time: 1 hour

slow burn martini

2 ounces premium vodka
$\frac{1}{2}$ ounce vermouth
5 drops Original TABASCO® brand Pepper Sauce
1 slice jalapeño pepper

Place 4 to 5 ice cubes in cocktail shaker. Pour vodka and vermouth over ice; cover and shake. Strain into chilled martini glass. Stir in TABASCO® Sauce; garnish with jalapeño. *Makes 1 martini*

classic bloody mary

(pictured at right)

1 quart tomato juice
1 cup vodka
1 tablespoon Worcestershire sauce
1 tablespoon fresh lime juice
½ teaspoon Original TABASCO® brand Pepper Sauce
  Lime slices for garnish (optional)
  Celery ribs for garnish (optional)

Combine all ingredients except garnishes in 2-quart pitcher. Stir well. Serve over ice. Garnish with lime slices or celery, if desired.

Makes 6 servings

peach bellinis

4 fresh California peaches, peeled and coarsely chopped
½ cup sugar
2 tablespoons lemon juice
¾ cup water
1 bottle (750 mL) chilled sweet sparkling wine
  Mint sprigs (optional)

Combine fruit, sugar, lemon juice and water in blender or food processor. Process until smooth.* To serve, pour about ¼ cup peach purée into 6- or 8-ounce stemmed glass. Slowly fill glass with sparkling wine. Stir to blend. Garnish with mint.   *Makes 10 servings*

If made ahead, cover and refrigerate for up to 3 hours. When ready to serve, continue as directed.

Favorite recipe from **California Tree Fruit Agreement**

homemade irish cream liqueur

2 cups whipping cream or coffee cream
1 (14-ounce) can EAGLE BRAND® Sweetened Condensed Milk (NOT evaporated milk)
1¼ to 1¾ cups Irish whiskey, brandy, rum, bourbon, Scotch or rye whiskey
2 tablespoons chocolate syrup
2 teaspoons instant coffee
1 teaspoon vanilla extract
½ teaspoon almond extract

1. In blender container, combine whipping cream, EAGLE BRAND®, whiskey, chocolate syrup, coffee, vanilla and almond extracts; blend until smooth.

2. Serve over ice. Store leftovers tightly covered in refrigerator.

Makes about 5 cups

Homemade Cream Liqueur: Omit Irish whiskey, chocolate syrup, coffee and extracts. Add 1¼ cups flavored liqueur (almond, coffee, orange or mint) to EAGLE BRAND® and cream. Proceed as directed above.

Tip: For a more blended flavor, store the homemade liqueur in the refrigerator for several hours before serving.

Prep Time: 5 minutes

mango-lime virgin margarita

(pictured at right)

1 large ripe mango, cubed (about 1$\frac{1}{4}$ to 1$\frac{1}{2}$ cups)
$\frac{1}{2}$ cup freshly squeezed lime juice
$\frac{1}{4}$ cup sugar
3 tablespoons orange juice
$\frac{1}{3}$ cup water
1 cup ice
2 lime slices

1. Combine mango, lime juice, sugar, orange juice, water and ice in blender. Blend until smooth.

2. Pour mixture into 2 salt-rimmed glasses.* Garnish with lime slices. Serve immediately.   *Makes 2 servings*

*See page 86.

celebration punch

1 can (46 fluid ounces) **DEL MONTE**® Pineapple Juice, chilled
1 can (46 fluid ounces) apricot nectar, chilled
1 cup orange juice
$\frac{1}{4}$ cup fresh lime juice
2 tablespoons grenadine
1 cup rum (optional)
Ice cubes

1. Combine all ingredients in punch bowl.

2. Garnish with pineapple wedges and lime slices, if desired.

Makes 16 servings

icy mimosas

(pictured at right)

3 cups frozen Tropic Ice, crushed (recipe follows)
3 cups ginger ale or Champagne
6 whole strawberries with stems

1. Spoon $\frac{1}{2}$ cup crushed Tropic Ice in each goblet.

2. Pour $\frac{1}{2}$ cup ginger ale over each serving. Garnish with 1 strawberry.

Makes 6 servings

tropic ice

4 cups tropical fruit juice, such as pineapple, orange and banana
1 can (12 ounces) ginger ale
$\frac{3}{4}$ cup frozen white grape juice concentrate
$\frac{1}{2}$ cup dry white wine, such as chardonnay (see Note)

1. Place all ingredients in gallon resealable freezer plastic bag. Place in freezer overnight or until frozen.

2. To serve, pound bag with meat mallet to break up. Freeze leftovers up to 1 month.

Makes 10 cups

Note: The alcohol in the wine keeps the mixture from freezing rock hard. The mixture will be harder if you do not use wine. Thaw slightly before breaking up. Or, chop the ice in a food processor to make a slush.

cranberry-lime margarita punch

(pictured at right)

6 cups water
1 container (12 ounces) frozen cranberry juice cocktail
$\frac{1}{2}$ cup fresh lime juice
$\frac{1}{4}$ cup EQUAL® SPOONFUL*
2 cups ice cubes
1 cup diet ginger ale or tequila
1 lime, sliced

May substitute 6 packets EQUAL® sweetener.

• Combine water, cranberry juice, lime juice and Equal® in punch bowl; stir until Equal® dissolves.

• Stir in ice cubes, diet ginger ale and sliced lime; garnish with fresh cranberries if desired.   *Makes 10 servings*

mimosa cocktail

1 bottle (750 mL) champagne, chilled
3 cups Florida orange juice, chilled

Combine equal parts of champagne and orange juice in champagne glasses. Serve immediately.   *Makes 12 servings*

Favorite recipe from **Florida Department of Citrus**

mango margarita

(pictured at top right)

$^1/_2$ cup **MAUNA LA'I® ¡Mango Mango!® Juice Drink**
1 ounce **tequila**
   Dash **ROSE'S® Triple Sec**
   Dash **ROSE'S® Lime Juice**
   Lime wedge, as needed
   Ice, as needed

Combine Mauna La'i ¡Mango Mango! Juice Drink, tequila, triple sec and lime juice in shaker with ice. Pour into salt-rimmed margarita glass. Garnish with lime.   *Makes 1 drink*

kiwi margarita

(pictured at far right)

$3^1/_2$ ounces **MR & MRS T® Margarita Mix**
2 ripe **kiwi, peeled**
1 cup **strawberry sorbet**
$1^1/_2$ ounces **white rum**
2 ounces **club soda**
1 **lime, sliced**
   MR & MRS T® Margarita Salt (optional)

Blend first 5 ingredients in blender on low speed until smooth.* Coat rim of glass with lime and dip in margarita salt, if desired. Pour into glass.
Makes 1 serving

Be careful not to blend too long, as crushed kiwi seeds taste bitter.

daiquiri

(pictured on page 213)

¾ cup **MAUNA LA'I® iMango Mango!® Juice Drink**
3 tablespoons rum
1 tablespoon **ROSE'S® Lime Juice**
1 teaspoon sugar
Ice, as needed

Combine Mauna La'i iMango Mango! Juice Drink, rum, lime juice and sugar in shaker with ice. Pour into tall glass filled with ice.   *Makes 1 drink*

nectarine sunrise

4 fresh California nectarines
1 can (6 ounces) frozen limeade concentrate
⅔ cup tequila
2 to 3 cups crushed ice
½ cup grenadine syrup
Fresh mint sprigs

Slice 1 nectarine; set aside for garnish. Coarsely chop remaining nectarines. In blender, combine chopped nectarines, limeade and tequila; purée until smooth. Gradually add crushed ice, blending until slushy and mixture measures 5 cups. Place 1 tablespoon grenadine syrup in each of 8 stemmed glasses. Add nectarine mixture. Top each with mint sprig and nectarine slice on side of glass. Serve immediately.   *Makes 8 servings*

Favorite recipe from **California Tree Fruit Agreement**

virgin mojito

2 bunches fresh mint (about 20 sprigs)
1 cup water
1¼ cups sugar, divided
1 cup freshly squeezed lime juice (about 8 limes)
2 limes, cut into wedges
4 (8-ounce) lowball glasses
Ice cubes
2 cups sparkling water

1. Place 8 sprigs mint into small bowl; set aside.

2. Combine water and 1 cup sugar in small saucepan. Stir over medium heat until sugar dissolves and syrup becomes clear. Bring syrup to simmer; simmer 1 minute. Pour hot syrup over mint in bowl. Stir in lime juice, mashing mint against side of bowl with wooden spoon to bruise mint and release flavor. Let mixture steep 1 hour; strain into pitcher. Discard remaining mint. Chill until ready to serve.

3. Rub lime wedge around rims of glasses. Pour remaining ¼ cup sugar into small bowl; dip rims of glasses in sugar. Place 3 sprigs fresh mint into each glass. Fill glasses with ice cubes. Pour glasses half full with chilled lime mixture. Top off each glass with sparkling water. Stir gently with swizzle stick or straw. Garnish with lime slice. *Makes 4 (1-cup) servings*

white sangria

(pictured at right)

2 oranges, cut into $1/4$-inch slices
2 lemons, cut into $1/4$-inch slices
$1/2$ cup sugar
2 bottles dry, fruity white wine (such as Pinot Grigio), chilled
$1/2$ cup peach schnapps
3 ripe peaches, pit removed and cut into wedges
2 cups ice cubes (about 16 cubes)

1. Place orange and lemon slices in large punch bowl. Pour sugar over orange and lemon slices. Lightly mash until sugar dissolves and fruit begins to break down.

2. Stir in wine, peach schnapps and peaches. Refrigerate at least 2 hours or up to 10. Add ice cubes just before serving.   *Makes 8 to 10 servings*

piña colada punch

5 cups DOLE® Pineapple Juice, divided
1 can (15 ounces) real cream of coconut
1 liter lemon-lime soda
2 limes, divided
$1^{1}/_{2}$ cups light rum (optional)
    Ice cubes
    Fresh mint sprigs

• Chill all ingredients.

• Blend 2 cups pineapple juice and cream of coconut in blender. Combine puréed mixture with remaining 3 cups pineapple juice, soda, juice of 1 lime, rum and ice. Garnish with 1 sliced lime and mint sprigs.

Makes 15 servings

Holiday
specials

cranberry-pineapple punch

(pictured on page 219)

2$\frac{1}{2}$ cups cranberry juice, chilled
2 cups pineapple juice, chilled
$\frac{1}{2}$ teaspoon almond extract
2$\frac{1}{2}$ cups ginger ale, chilled
Ice cubes

1. Combine cranberry juice, pineapple juice and almond extract in large pitcher. Gently stir in ginger ale.

2. Serve over ice cubes.   *Makes 7 cups or about 9 servings*

holiday orange eggnog

1 container (8 ounces) refrigerated egg substitute to equal 4 eggs (1 cup)
$\frac{1}{3}$ cup sugar
2 teaspoons ground nutmeg
$\frac{1}{4}$ teaspoon ground cinnamon
2 cups cold milk
1 pint regular or low-fat frozen vanilla yogurt, softened
Juice of 3 SUNKIST® oranges (1 cup), chilled
$\frac{1}{2}$ to 1 cup rum, bourbon or brandy (or any combination)
Freshly grated SUNKIST® orange peel
Additional ground nutmeg

In large bowl, combine egg substitute, sugar, 2 teaspoons nutmeg and cinnamon; whisk well to dissolve sugar. Whisk in milk, yogurt, orange juice and rum. (If made ahead and chilled, whisk well before serving.) Garnish each serving with orange peel and dash of nutmeg.

Makes about 6 cups, 8 (6-ounce) or 12 (4-ounce) servings

festive cranberry cream punch

Cranberry Ice Ring (recipe follows) or ice
1 (14-ounce) can EAGLE BRAND® Sweetened Condensed Milk (NOT
    evaporated milk)
1 (12-ounce) can frozen cranberry juice cocktail concentrate, thawed
1 cup cranberry-flavored liqueur (optional)
Red food coloring (optional)
2 (1-liter) bottles club soda or ginger ale, chilled

1. Prepare Cranberry Ice Ring one day in advance.

2. In punch bowl, combine EAGLE BRAND®, cranberry concentrate, liqueur
(optional) and food coloring (optional).

3. Just before serving, add club soda and Cranberry Ice Ring or ice. Store
punch tightly covered in refrigerator.   *Makes about 3 quarts punch*

cranberry ice ring

2 cups cranberry juice cocktail
1$\frac{1}{2}$ cups water
$\frac{3}{4}$ cup cranberries and lime slices or mint leaves

1. Combine cranberry juice cocktail and water in large bowl. Pour $\frac{1}{2}$ cup
cranberry mixture in 1$\frac{1}{2}$-quart ring mold.

2. Arrange cranberries and lime slices or mint leaves in mold; freeze.

3. Add remaining 3 cups cranberry liquid to mold; freeze overnight.
                                        Makes 1 ice ring

creamy holiday mocha

(pictured at right)

1 can (14 ounces) sweetened condensed milk
1 cup water
1 cup espresso or strong brewed coffee
2 tablespoons unsweetened cocoa powder
$\frac{1}{2}$ teaspoon ground cinnamon
   Dash salt
$\frac{1}{2}$ teaspoon vanilla (optional)
   Whipped cream

1. Whisk condensed milk, water, espresso, cocoa, cinnamon and salt in large saucepan over medium heat until heated through until well blended. Remove from heat; whisk in vanilla until frothy.

2. Serve hot. Garnish with whipped cream. *Makes 4 servings*

Prep Time: **5 minutes**

pumpkin spice smoothie

$2\frac{1}{2}$ cups frozen vanilla yogurt
1 cup canned pumpkin
2 tablespoons packed brown sugar
1 tablespoon honey
1 teaspoon ground pumpkin pie spice
$\frac{1}{2}$ teaspoon ground nutmeg, plus extra for garnish
1 cup cubed or crushed ice

1. Place all ingredients in blender. Blend until smooth, stopping once to scrape down sides.

2. Pour smoothie into 4 glasses. Sprinkle with ground nutmeg. Serve immediately. *Makes 4 servings*

hot mulled cider

(pictured at right)

  1 orange
  1 lemon
12 whole cloves
  6 cups apple cider
$1/3$ cup sugar
  3 cinnamon sticks
12 whole allspice berries

1. Poke 6 evenly spaced holes in ring around orange and lemon with point of wooden skewer. Insert whole cloves into holes. Cut slice out of orange to include all cloves. Cut remainder of orange into thin slices. Repeat procedure with lemon.

2. Combine all ingredients in medium saucepan. Bring to a simmer over medium heat. *Do not boil.* Reduce heat to low; cook 5 minutes.

3. Pour cider through strainer into mugs. Discard fruit and seasonings.

Makes 6 cups

kahlúa® & eggnog

  1 quart dairy eggnog
$3/4$ cup KAHLÚA® Liqueur
    Whipped cream
    Ground nutmeg

Combine eggnog and Kahlúa® in $1^{1}/_{2}$-quart pitcher. Pour into punch cups. Top with whipped cream. Sprinkle with nutmeg.

Makes about 8 servings

festive holiday punch

(pictured at right)

8 cups MOTT'S® Apple Juice
8 cups cranberry juice cocktail
2 red apples, sliced
2 cups cranberries
3 liters lemon-lime soda
   Ice cubes, as needed

Pour apple and cranberry juices into punch bowl. Fifteen minutes before serving, add apple slices, cranberries, soda and ice. Do not stir.

Makes 24 servings

coconut snowball cocoa

1 pint vanilla ice cream
1 cup flaked coconut
$1/2$ cup unsweetened cocoa powder
1 quart milk
$3/4$ to 1 cup cream of coconut
$1/2$ cup dark rum (optional)
1 teaspoon coconut extract
$1/2$ cup chocolate syrup (optional)
8 maraschino cherries (optional)

1. Scoop ice cream into 8 small balls; immediately roll in coconut. Place on waxed paper-lined baking sheet; freeze until ready to use.

2. Whisk cocoa into milk in large saucepan. Stir in cream of coconut, rum, if desired, and coconut extract. Bring to a simmer over medium-high heat. Pour into 8 large heatproof mugs.

3. Float ice cream balls in cocoa. Drizzle each ice cream ball with chocolate syrup and top with cherry, if desired.

Makes 8 servings

wassail bowl

Ingredients

Dried apple slices
Colored sugar
$3/4$ cup water
$3/4$ cup granulated sugar
$1/2$ teaspoon ground ginger
$1/4$ teaspoon ground nutmeg
1 small cinnamon stick
3 whole cloves
3 whole allspice
3 coriander seeds
3 cardamom seeds (optional)
3 cups ale or wine
$2 1/4$ cups dry sherry
$1/3$ cup cognac

Supplies

Tiny cookie cutters

1. Cut dried apple slices into festive shapes with cookie cutters or sharp knife. Moisten with water and coat with colored sugar. Set aside.

2. Combine $3/4$ cup water, granulated sugar and spices in large saucepan. Bring to a boil. Cover; reduce heat and simmer 5 minutes.

3. Stir in ale, sherry and cognac; heat just to simmering. *Do not boil.* Strain into heatproof pitcher or punch bowl. Float apple slices in punch.

Makes 12 servings (about 4 ounces each)

mexican coffee with chocolate and cinnamon

6 cups water
$1/2$ cup ground dark roast coffee
2 cinnamon sticks
1 cup half-and-half
$1/3$ cup chocolate syrup
$1/4$ cup packed dark brown sugar
1 teaspoon vanilla
1 cup whipping cream
$1/4$ cup powdered sugar
$1/2$ teaspoon vanilla
Ground cinnamon

1. Place water in drip coffee maker. Place coffee and cinnamon sticks in coffee filter. Combine half-and-half, chocolate syrup, brown sugar and vanilla in coffee pot. Place coffee pot with cream mixture in coffee maker. Brew coffee; coffee will drip into chocolate cream mixture.

2. Meanwhile, beat whipping cream in medium bowl with electric mixer at high speed until soft peaks form. Add powdered sugar and vanilla; beat until stiff peaks form. Pour coffee into individual coffee cups; top with dollop of whipped cream. Sprinkle with ground cinnamon.

Makes 10 to 12 servings

Drink mixes

spiced raspberry tea mix

1 cup sugar

³/₄ cup instant unsweetened tea

4 packets (0.23 ounce each) raspberry-flavored unsweetened
  drink mix

2 tablespoons lemonade drink mix

1 teaspoon ground cardamom

1 teaspoon ground cinnamon

1 teaspoon ground ginger

¹/₂ teaspoon allspice

1. Combine all ingredients in medium bowl; mix well. Spoon mixture into 1-pint food storage jar, packing down firmly.

2. Seal jar; store in cool dry place up to 2 months.

Makes 1 (1-pint) jar (20 to 25 servings)

spiced raspberry tea

(pictured on page 233)

1 to 1¹/₂ tablespoons Spiced Raspberry Tea Mix

6 ounces boiling water

  Fresh raspberries (optional)

  Fresh orange slice (optional)

  Sprig of fresh mint (optional)

1. Spoon tea mix into cup or mug. Pour water over mix. Stir to dissolve.

2. Serve hot or over ice. Garnish with raspberries, orange slice and mint.

Makes 1 serving

mango and mint tea mix

¾ cup loose English breakfast tea leaves
¼ cup minced dried mango
¼ cup dried mint leaves

1. Combine all ingredients in medium bowl; mix well. Spoon mixture into ½-pint food storage jar with tight-fitting lid.

2. Seal jar. Store in cool dry place up to 2 months.

Makes 1 (½-pint) jar

mango and mint tea

1 tablespoon Mango and Mint Tea Mix
1 cup boiling water
Honey (optional)
Lemon wedge (optional)

1. Press 1 rounded tablespoon tea mix into tea infuser spoon or tea ball. Place in mug. Add water; let stand 4 minutes.

2. Remove tea infuser. Serve with honey and lemon.   *Makes 1 serving*

Note: You can also brew tea using tea filters which are available in many coffee shops.

chai tea latte mix

1 cup powdered nondairy creamer
$3/4$ cup instant unsweetened tea
$1/4$ cup granulated sugar
3 tablespoons nonfat dry milk
2 tablespoons packed brown sugar
$1/2$ teaspoon ground allspice
$1/2$ teaspoon ground cardamom
$1/2$ teaspoon ground cinnamon
$1/2$ teaspoon ground cloves
$1/2$ teaspoon ground ginger

1. Combine all ingredients in medium bowl; mix well. Spoon mixture into 1-pint food storage jar, packing down firmly.

2. Seal jar; store in cool dry place up to 2 months.   *Makes 1 (1-pint) jar*

chai tea latte

(pictured at right)

2 tablespoons Chai Tea Latte Mix
1 cup hot milk
$1/2$ to 1 teaspoon honey

Spoon Latte Mix into cup or mug. Add hot milk; stir to dissolve. Sweeten with honey to taste. Serve hot.   *Makes 1 serving*

cranberry-apricot tea mix

6 ounces dried cranberries, chopped
4 ounces Mediterranean or Turkish dried apricots, chopped
2 (3-inch) cinnamon sticks, broken into small pieces
16 to 20 whole cloves

1. Combine all ingredients in medium bowl; mix well. Spoon into 1-pint food storage jar with tight-fitting lid, packing down firmly.

2. Seal jar; store in cool dry place up to 2 months.   *Makes 1 (1-pint) jar*

cranberry-apricot tea

(pictured at right)

1 jar Cranberry-Apricot Tea Mix
Honey or sugar (optional)
Fresh mint sprig (optional)

1. Bring 2 quarts water to a boil in large saucepan over high heat. Stir tea mixture into boiling water. Reduce heat and simmer, covered, 10 minutes.

2. Remove from heat; let tea steep, covered, about 10 minutes. Strain through mesh strainer into mug or cup, pressing fruit against strainer with back of spoon. Serve with honey, if desired. Garnish with mint.

Makes about 6 servings

Variation: Pour cooled tea over ice and top with a splash of sparkling water. Garnish with orange slice.

mocha coffee mix

²⁄₃ cup unsweetened cocoa powder
½ cup nonfat dry milk
½ cup powdered sugar
⅓ cup granulated sugar
¼ cup instant coffee granules
1½ teaspoons ground cinnamon
½ teaspoon ground nutmeg

1. Combine all ingredients in medium bowl; mix well. Spoon into 1-pint food storage jar with tight-fitting lid, packing down firmly.

2. Seal jar; store in cool dry place up to 2 months.   *Makes 1 (1-pint) jar*

mocha coffee

(pictured at right)

1 to 2 tablespoons Mocha Coffee Mix
1 cup hot milk

1. Spoon Coffee Mix into cup or mug. Add hot milk; stir to dissolve.

2. Serve hot.   *Makes 1 serving*

bloody mary mix

1 quart (4 cups) vegetable juice cocktail
2 tablespoons **LEA & PERRINS®** Worcestershire Sauce
1 tablespoon fresh lime or lemon juice
$\frac{1}{4}$ teaspoon granulated sugar
$\frac{1}{4}$ teaspoon pepper
$\frac{1}{4}$ teaspoon hot pepper sauce
$\frac{1}{8}$ teaspoon garlic powder

In pitcher, thoroughly combine all ingredients, cover and chill. Serve over ice. Garnish with celery stalks and lime wedges, if desired.

Makes about 1 quart

Bloody Mary Cocktail: **Add 3 or 4 parts Bloody Mary Mix to 1 part vodka.**

Give classic drinks such as lemonade and tea a new twist with fresh herbs. Add herb sprigs to hot or cold drinks or steep herbs in simple syrup for a more intense flavor. Lemon verbena or thyme taste great with lemonade. Try the recipe on page 243 with basil and dried lemon peel.

lemon and basil tea mix

$^3/_4$ **cup plus 2 tablespoons loose English breakfast tea leaves**
2 tablespoons dried lemon peel
2 tablespoons dried basil

1. Combine tea, lemon peel and basil in medium bowl; mix well. Pour into $^1/_2$-pint food storage jar with tight-fitting lid.

2. Seal jar. Store in cool dry place up to 2 months.

Makes 1 ($^1/_2$-pint) jar

lemon and basil tea

1 tablespoon Lemon and Basil Tea Mix
1 cup boiling water
  Honey (optional)
  Lemon wedge (optional)

1. Press tea mix into tea infuser or tea ball. Place in heatproof mug; add water. Let stand 4 minutes.

2. Remove tea infuser. Serve with honey and lemon, if desired.

Makes 1 serving

Note: You can also brew tea using tea filters available in many coffee shops.

spiced-up cocoa mix

    1 cup granulated sugar
    ½ cup unsweetened cocoa powder
    1 tablespoon all-purpose flour
    2 teaspoons ground cinnamon
 1½ teaspoons ground cloves
    ½ teaspoon chile powder
    ½ teaspoon salt
    ¼ teaspoon ground allspice
    ½ cup (about 30) mini marshmallows

1. Combine all ingredients except marshmallows in medium bowl; mix well. Spoon into 1-pint food storage jar with tight-fitting lid, packing down firmly. Place marshmallows in resealable food storage bag; place bag in jar. (Add or remove marshmallows as space allows.)

2. Seal jar; store in cool dry place up to 2 months.   *Makes 1 (1-pint) jar*

spiced-up cocoa

(pictured at right)

    ⅓ cup water
    ¾ cup Spiced-Up Cocoa Mix
    4 cups milk
    ¾ teaspoon vanilla

1. Set aside mini marshmallows. Bring water to a boil in large saucepan over high heat. Whisk in Spiced-Up Cocoa Mix until dissolved. Reduce heat to medium, stirring 1 to 2 minutes or until thick and smooth.

2. Add milk and vanilla; heat until hot, stirring constantly. *Do not boil.* Pour cocoa into 4 mugs; top with mini marshmallows. Serve hot.

Makes 4 servings

mulling spices for hot spiced cider

1 package 100% cotton cheesecloth
12 cinnamon sticks, broken into 1-inch pieces
$\frac{1}{4}$ cup allspice berries (about $\frac{3}{4}$ ounce)
$\frac{1}{4}$ cup whole cloves (about $\frac{3}{4}$ ounce)
1 tablespoon grated dried lemon peel
1 tablespoon grated dried orange peel
1 tablespoon ground cardamom
1 tablespoon ground nutmeg
6 (12-inch) lengths poultry twine or food-safe string

1. Cut 6 (6-inch) squares of cheesecloth (double thickness); set aside. Combine remaining ingredients in small mixing bowl. Divide mixture equally among cheesecloth squares, about $\frac{1}{4}$ cup per square. Bring corners of squares together and tuck in any loose edges. Tie each bag tightly with twine. Layer spice bags in decorative container with a tight-fitting lid.

2. Seal jar; store in cool dry place up to 2 months.   *Makes 6 spice bags*

hot spiced cider

(pictured at right)

1 quart apple cider
1 Mulling Spice Bag

1. Heat apple cider and mulling spice bag in large saucepan over medium heat until cider 10 minutes or until hot. *Do not boil.*

2. Serve in mugs.   *Makes 1 quart*

Acknowledgments

The publisher would like to thank the companies and organizations listed below for the use of their recipes and photographs in this publication.

California Tree Fruit Agreement

Campbell Soup Company

Chilean Fresh Fruit Association

Cream of Wheat® Cereal

Del Monte Corporation

Dole Food Company, Inc.

Domino® Foods, Inc.

EAGLE BRAND®

Equal® sweetener

Florida Department of Citrus

Heinz North America

The Hershey Company

The Kahlúa® Liqueur trademark is used under permission from Malibu Kahlua International, White Plains, N.Y.

© Mars, Incorporated 2008

Mauna La'i® is a registered trademark of Mott's, LLP

McIlhenny Company (TABASCO® brand Pepper Sauce)

Mott's® is a registered trademark of Mott's, LLP

Mr & Mrs T® is a registered trademark of Mott's, LLP

National Honey Board

Nestlé USA

Peanut Advisory Board

The Sugar Association, Inc.

Reprinted with permission of Sunkist Growers, Inc. All Rights Reserved.

Unilever

A

Almond Milk Tea with Tapioca, 8
Anti-Stress Smoothie, 102
Apple
  Apple Pie Shake, 170
  Berry Soy-Cream Blend, 84
  Cranberry Pear Ginger Smoothie, 98
  Festive Holiday Punch, 226
  Frozen Apple Slushies, 158
  Hot Mulled Cider, 224
  Hot Spiced Cider, 246
  Hot Tropics Sipper, 178
  Mixed Berry Smoothie, 94
  Quick Apple Punch, 166
  Red Hot Apple Mugs, 135
  Sparkling Apple Punch, 164
  Sparkling Ginger-Apple Cider, 136
  Sparkling Ginger-Apple Float, 136
  Tofu, Fruit & Veggie Smoothies, 146
  Tropical Tea-Mulled Cider, 28
  Vermont Maple Smoothie, 162
Apricot
  Apricot Peachy Chillers, 148
  Celebration Punch, 206
  Cranberry-Apricot Tea, 238
  Cranberry-Apricot Tea Mix, 238
  Hot Tropics Sipper, 178
  Soy Apricot Peachy Chillers, 148

B

Banana
  Anti-Stress Smoothie, 102
  Banana Berry Smoothie, 72
  Banana-Coconut "Cream Pie"
    Smoothie, 152
  Banana-Pineapple Breakfast Shake,
    140
  Banana Smoothie, 156
  Banana Split Shakes, 58
  Chocolate Covered Banana Slushy,
    47
  Frozen Florida Monkey Malts, 170
  Fruit 'n Juice Breakfast Shake, 168

Banana (continued)
  "Hot" Chocolate Smoothie, 52
  Island Delight Smoothie, 175
  Jungle Juice, 188
  Peachy Keen Smoothie, 134
  Soy Milk Smoothie, 150
  Spiced Passion Fruit-Yogurt Starter,
    138
  Strawberry Banana Coconut
    Smoothie, 192
  Tea Colada, 12
  Tofu Peanut Butter Smoothie, 160
  Triple Berry Blast, 86
  Wake-Me-Up Breakfast Smoothie, 73
  Wow Watermelon Smoothie, 164
Bavarian Wild Berry Cosmopolitan, 201
Berry Berry Mango Smoothie, 76
Berry Soy-Cream Blend, 84
Black Forest Smoothie, 88
Black Pearl Hot 'n Spicy Chocolate
    Tea, 54
Bloody Mary Cocktail, 242
Bloody Mary Mix, 242
Blueberry
  Anti-Stress Smoothie, 102
  Blueberry Cherry "Cheesecake"
    Smoothie, 82
  Blueberry Pineapple Smoothie, 92
  Chocolate-Blueberry Soy Shake, 96
  Fruit 'n Juice Breakfast Shake, 168
  Mixed Berry Smoothie, 94
  Powerful Pomegranate Smoothie,
    73
Bubbling Raspberry Coolers, 76

C

Cantaloupe Smoothie, 158
Carrot Cake Smoothie, 148
Celebration Punch, 206
Chai Tea, 20
Chai Tea Latte, 236
Chai Tea Latte Mix, 236
Champagne: Mimosa Cocktail, 210

Cherry
Black Forest Smoothie, 88
Blueberry Cherry "Cheesecake"
    Smoothie, 82
Cherry Chocolate Frosty, 64
Chilled Café Latte, 40
Chilled Lemon Sunset, 116
Chipotle Chili-Spiked Mocha Slush,
    32
Chocolate, 44–69
Black Forest Smoothie, 88
Chipotle Chili-Spiked Mocha Slush,
    32
Chocolate-Blueberry Soy Shake, 96
Coconut Snowball Cocoa, 226
Iced Mexican Coffee, 42
Mexican Coffee with Chocolate and
    Cinnamon, 230
Mocha Coffee, 240
Mocha Coffee Mix, 240
Mocha Madness, 33
Mocha Shake, 40
Spiced-Up Cocoa, 244
Spiced-Up Cocoa Mix, 244
Tiramisu Smoothie, 38
Citrus Cooler, 112
Citrus Punch, 107
Classic Bloody Mary, 201
Coconut
Banana-Coconut "Cream Pie"
    Smoothie, 152
Coconut Cream Pie Chill, 68
Coconut Snowball Cocoa, 226
Mandarin Orange, Coconut and
    Lime Cooler, 128
Melon Bubble Tea, 6
Mocha Colada, 34
Piña Colada Punch, 216
Strawberry Banana Coconut
    Smoothie, 192
Thai Coconut Iced Tea, 12
Toasted Coco Colada, 184
Tropical Breeze Smoothies, 196

Coffee, 30–43
Creamy Holiday Mocha, 222
Mexican Coffee with Chocolate and
    Cinnamon, 230
Mocha Coffee, 240
Mocha Coffee Mix, 240
Cranberry
Cranberry-Apricot Tea, 238
Cranberry-Apricot Tea Mix, 238
Cranberry Ice Ring, 221
Cranberry-Lime Margarita Punch, 210
Cranberry Lime Ricky, 72
Cranberry 'n' Lemon Tea Punch, 10
Cranberry Orange Smoothie, 114
Cranberry Pear Ginger Smoothie, 98
Cranberry-Pineapple Punch, 220
Festive Cranberry Cream Punch, 221
Festive Holiday Punch, 226
Frozen Apple Slushies, 158
Mulled Cranberry Tea, 24
Quick Apple Punch, 166
Sparkling Tangerine-Cranberry Green
    Tea, 28
Creamy Holiday Mocha, 222
Creamy Hot Chocolate, 50
Cuban Batido, 194
Cuban Guava Punch, 174

D
Dreamsicle Smoothie, 106
Drinking Chocolate, 64

E
Egg Cream, 54
Espresso Shake, 36

F
Festive Citrus Punch, 130
Festive Cranberry Cream Punch, 221
Festive Holiday Punch, 226
Frosty Five-Spice Coffee Shake, 32
Frozen Apple Slushies, 158
Frozen Florida Monkey Malts, 170

Frozen Hot Chocolate, 62
Frozen Rainbow Bubblers, 142
Frozen Watermelon Whip, 150
Fruit 'n Juice Breakfast Shake, 168

G
Gingerbread with Lemon Sauce Shake,
    112
Ginger-Cucumber Limeade, 118
Ginger-Lime Iced Green Tea, 10
Ginger-Pineapple Spritzer, 160
Grapefruit
    Citrus Punch, 107
    Festive Citrus Punch, 130
    Passion Potion, 120
Grape Roughie, 134
Green Tea Citrus Smoothie, 26
Green Tea Lychee Frappé, 22

H
Holiday Orange Eggnog, 220
Homemade Cream Liqueur, 204
Homemade Irish Cream Liqueur, 204
Honey Coffee Cooler, 33
Honeyed Lemonade, 128
Honey Lemonade, 118
Honey Orange Marys, 120
Horchata Shake, 180
"Hot" Chocolate Smoothie, 52
Hot Chocolate Tea, 48
Hot Mulled Cider, 224
Hot Spiced Cider, 246
Hot Spiced Tea, 16
Hot Tropics Sipper, 178

I
Iced Almond Chai Tea Latte, 16
Iced Café Latte, 36
Iced Mexican Coffee, 42
Icy Fruit Tea, 7
Icy Mimosas, 208
Irish Cream Iced Cappuccino, 46
Island Delight Smoothie, 175

J
Jungle Juice, 188

K
Kahlúa® & Coffee, 42
Kahlúa® & Eggnog, 224
Kahlúa® Hot Spiced Apple Cider, 204
Kahlúa® Parisian Coffee, 200
Key Lime Pie Refresher, 106
Kiwi
    Kiwi Margarita, 212
    Kiwi Strawberry Smoothie, 88
    Soy Kiwi Strawberry Smoothie, 88

L
Lemon
    Chilled Lemon Sunset, 116
    Citrus Punch, 107
    Cranberry 'n' Lemon Tea Punch, 10
    Gingerbread with Lemon Sauce
        Shake, 112
    Green Tea Citrus Smoothie, 26
    Honeyed Lemonade, 128
    Honey Lemonade, 118
    Hot Tropics Sipper, 178
    Lemon Basil Smoothie, 108
    Lemon Chiffon Cooler, 124
    Lemon Herbal Iced Tea, 18
    Lemon-Lime Watermelon Agua
        Fresca, 180
    Lemon-Raspberry Brain Freeze, 82
    Lemon Sangrita Punch, 190
    Mulled Cranberry Tea, 24
    Peach-Lemon Frost, 110
    Pineapple-Lemonade Pizzazz, 154
    Pineapple-Mint Lemonade, 126
    Pink Lemonade, 128
    Real Old-Fashioned Lemonade, 128
    Rockin' Raspberry Refresher, 98
    Summer Spritzer, 126
Lime
    Celebration Punch, 206
    Citrus Punch, 107

Lime (continued)

Cranberry-Lime Margarita Punch, 210
Cranberry Lime Ricky, 72
Cuban Guava Punch, 174
Ginger-Cucumber Limeade, 118
Ginger-Lime Iced Green Tea, 10
Icy Fruit Tea, 7
Key Lime Pie Refresher, 106
Lemon-Lime Watermelon Agua
    Fresca, 180
Mandarin Orange, Coconut and Lime
    Cooler, 128
Mango-Lime Virgin Margarita, 206
Mango Smoothie, 186
Nectarine Sunrise, 214
Piña Colada Punch, 216
Pineapple Agua Fresca, 192
Raspberry Mint Cooler, 84
Sangrita, 175, 196
Sparkling Strawberry-Lime Shakes,
    100
Strawberry Limeade, 122
Strawberry-Mango Daiquiri Punch,
    200
Virgin Mojito, 215

M

Mandarin Orange, Coconut and Lime
    Cooler, 128
Mandarin Orange Smoothie, 110
"M&M's"® Brain Freezer Shake, 48
Mango

Berry Berry Mango Smoothie, 76
Daiquiri, 214
Island Delight Smoothie, 175
Mango and Mint Tea, 235
Mango and Mint Tea Mix, 235
Mango-Ginger Smoothie, 188
Mango-Lime Virgin Margarita,
    206
Mango Margarita, 212
Mango Smoothie, 186
Mango Tea Frost, 26

Mango (continued)

Strawberry-Mango Daiquiri Punch,
    200
Tropical Breeze Smoothies, 196
Margarita

Cranberry-Lime Margarita Punch,
    210
Kiwi Margarita, 212
Mango-Lime Margarita, 206
Mango Margarita, 212
Melon Bubble Tea, 6
Melon Cooler, 186
Mexican Coffee with Chocolate and
    Cinnamon, 230
Mimosa Cocktail, 210
Mint Chocolate Chip Milkshakes, 60
Mint-Green Tea Coolers, 14
Mint Tea Juleps, 21
Mint-Turtle Tornado, 66
Mixed Berry Smoothie, 94
Mocha Coffee, 240
Mocha Coffee Mix, 240
Mocha Colada, 34
Mocha Cooler, 36
Mocha Madness, 33
Mocha Shake, 40
Mulled Cranberry Tea, 24
Mysterious Chocolate Mint Coolers, 56
Mystic Chocolate Mint Cooler, 68

N

Nectarine Sunrise, 214

O

Orange

Cantaloupe Smoothie, 158
Celebration Punch, 206
Chilled Lemon Sunset, 116
Citrus Cooler, 112
Citrus Punch, 107
Cranberry Orange Smoothie, 114
Cuban Batido, 194
Cuban Guava Punch, 174

Orange *(continued)*
  Dreamsicle Smoothie, 106
  Holiday Orange Eggnog, 220
  Honey Orange Marys, 120
  Hot Tropics Sipper, 178
  Icy Fruit Tea, 7
  Mandarin Orange, Coconut and Lime
    Cooler, 128
  Mandarin Orange Smoothie, 110
  Melon Bubble Tea, 6
  Mimosa Cocktail, 210
  Orange Iced Tea, 18
  Peachy Keen Smoothie, 134
  Sangrita, 175, 196
  Sparkling Tropical Fruit Combo, 184
  Strawberry Delights, 168
  Tofu, Fruit & Veggie Smoothies, 146
  Tofu Orange Dream, 126

P

Papaya: Sparkling Apple Punch, 164
Passion Potion, 120
Peach
  Apricot Peachy Chillers, 148
  Cranberry Orange Smoothie, 114
  Mango-Ginger Smoothie, 188
  Peach Bellinis, 202
  Peach-Lemon Frost, 110
  Peach Smoothie, 146
  Peachy Chocolate Yogurt Shake, 56
  Peachy Keen Smoothie, 134
  Pineapple-Lemonade Pizzazz, 154
  Raspberry Peach Perfection
    Smoothie, 80
  Southern-Style Peach Tea, 21
  Soy Apricot Peachy Chillers, 148
  White Sangria, 216
Piña Colada Punch, 216
Pineapple
  Banana-Coconut "Cream Pie"
    Smoothie, 152
  Banana-Pineapple Breakfast Shake,
    140

Pineapple *(continued)*
  Blueberry Pineapple Smoothie, 92
  Celebration Punch, 206
  Citrus Cooler, 112
  Coconut Cream Pie Chill, 68
  Cranberry-Pineapple Punch, 220
  Cuban Batido, 194
  Cuban Guava Punch, 174
  Festive Citrus Punch, 130
  Fruit 'n Juice Breakfast Shake, 168
  Ginger-Pineapple Spritzer, 160
  Guava Fruit Punch, 136
  Hot Tropics Sipper, 178
  Icy Fruit Tea, 7
  Island Delight Smoothie, 175
  Melon Cooler, 186
  Piña Colada Punch, 216
  Pineapple Agua Fresca, 192
  Pineapple-Lemonade Pizzazz, 154
  Pineapple-Mint Lemonade, 126
  Raspberry Mint Cooler, 84
  Summer Spritzer, 126
  Tea Colada, 12
  Tofu, Fruit & Veggie Smoothies, 146
  Tropical Breeze Smoothies, 196
  Tropic Ice, 208
  White Sangria, 187
Pink Lemonade, 128
Plum Purple Frappé, 138
Pomegranate
  Powerful Pomegranate Smoothie, 73
  Sparkling Pomegranate Gingerade,
    176
Pumpkin Spice Smoothie, 222

Q

Quick Apple Punch, 166

R

Raspberry
  Berry Berry Mango Smoothie, 76
  Bubbling Raspberry Coolers, 76
  Citrus Punch, 107

Raspberry (continued)
Lemon-Raspberry Brain Freeze, 82
Mixed Berry Smoothie, 94
Raspberry Chocolate Smoothie, 66
Raspberry Mint Cooler, 84
Raspberry Peach Perfection
  Smoothie, 80
Raspberry Soda Smoothie, 90
Raspberry Watermelon Slush, 166
Rockin' Raspberry Refresher, 98
Spiced Raspberry Tea, 234
Spiced Raspberry Tea Mix, 234
Real Old-Fashioned Lemonade, 128
Red Hot Apple Mugs, 136
Red Tea Harvest Strawberry Smoothie,
  96
Rockin' Raspberry Refresher, 98
Royal Hot Chocolate, 60
Rum
Daiquiri, 214
Holiday Orange Eggnog, 220
Kiwi Margarita, 212
Piña Colada Punch, 216
Strawberry-Mango Daiquiri Punch,
  200

S
Salt-Dipped Glasses, 86
Sangrita, 175, 196
Shakes
Apple Pie Shake, 170
Banana-Pineapple Breakfast Shake,
  140
Banana Split Shakes, 58
Chocolate Chip Cookie Milk Shake,
  58
Fruit 'n Juice Breakfast Shake, 168
Gingerbread with Lemon Sauce
  Shake, 112
"M&M's"® Brain Freezer Shake, 48
Mint Chocolate Chip Milkshakes,
  60
Peachy Chocolate Yogurt Shake, 56

Shakes (continued)
Peanut Butter & Jelly Shakes, 80
Strawberry & Chocolate Shake, 52
Sippable Gazpacho, 182
Slow Burn Martini, 201
Southern-Style Peach Tea, 21
Soy Apricot Peachy Chillers, 148
Soy Kiwi Strawberry Smoothie, 88
Soy Milk Smoothie, 150
Spanish Coffee, 38
Sparkling Apple Punch, 164
Sparkling Ginger-Apple Cider, 136
Sparkling Ginger-Apple Float, 136
Sparkling Pomegranate Gingerade, 176
Sparkling Strawberry Float, 78
Sparkling Strawberry-Lime Shakes, 100
Sparkling Tangerine-Cranberry Green
  Tea, 28
Sparkling Tropical Fruit Combo, 184
Spiced Passion Fruit-Yogurt Starter, 138
Spiced Raspberry Tea, 234
Spiced Raspberry Tea Mix, 234
Spiced-Up Cocoa, 244
Spiced-Up Cocoa Mix, 244
Strawberry
Apricot Peachy Chillers, 148
Banana Berry Smoothie, 72
Berry Berry Mango Smoothie, 76
Citrus Punch, 107
Icy Mimosas, 208
Island Delight Smoothie, 175
Jungle Juice, 188
Kiwi Margarita, 212
Kiwi Strawberry Smoothie, 88
Mixed Berry Smoothie, 94
Powerful Pomegranate Smoothie,
  73
Red Tea Harvest Strawberry
  Smoothie, 96
Soy Apricot Peachy Chillers, 148
Soy Kiwi Strawberry Smoothie, 88
Soy Milk Smoothie, 150
Sparkling Strawberry Float, 78

Strawberry *(continued)*
    Sparkling Strawberry-Lime Shakes, 100
    Spiced Passion Fruit-Yogurt Starter, 138
    Strawberry & Chocolate Shake, 52
    Strawberry Banana Coconut Smoothie, 192
    Strawberry Blast, 92
    Strawberry Cheesecake Smoothie, 74
    Strawberry Delights, 168
    Strawberry Limeade, 122
    Strawberry-Mango Daiquiri Punch, 200
    Triple Strawberry Smoothie, 102
    Wake-Me-Up Breakfast Smoothie, 73
    White Sangria, 187
    Wow Watermelon Smoothie, 164
Striped Grape Smoothie, 144
Sugar-Dipped Glasses, 86
Summer Spritzer, 126

T
Tea, 4–29
    Bavarian Wild Berry Cosmopolitan, 201
    Black Pearl Hot 'n Spicy Chocolate Tea, 54
    Chai Tea Latte, 236
    Chai Tea Latte Mix, 236
    Cranberry-Apricot Tea, 238
    Cranberry-Apricot Tea Mix, 238
    Frozen Watermelon Whip, 150
    Guava Fruit Punch, 136
    Hot Chocolate Tea, 48
    Lemon and Basil Tea, 243
    Lemon and Basil Tea Mix, 243
    Mango and Mint Tea, 235
    Mango and Mint Tea Mix, 235
    Spiced Raspberry Tea, 234
    Spiced Raspberry Tea Mix, 234

Tequila
    Mango Margarita, 212
    Nectarine Sunrise, 214
Thai Coconut Iced Tea, 12
Tiramisu Smoothie, 38
Toasted Coco Colada, 184
Tofu
    Berry Soy-Cream Blend, 84
    Tofu, Fruit & Veggie Smoothies, 146
    Tofu Orange Dream, 126
    Tofu Peanut Butter Smoothie, 160
Triple Berry Blast, 86
Triple Strawberry Smoothie, 102
Tropical Tea-Mulled Cider, 28
Tropic Ice, 208

V
Vanilla Caramel Truffle Latte, 14
Vermont Maple Smoothie, 162
Viennese Coffee, 34
Virgin Mojito, 215
Vodka
    Bavarian Wild Berry Cosmopolitan, 201
    Bloody Mary Cocktail, 242
    Classic Bloody Mary, 201
    Slow Burn Martini, 201

W
Wake-Me-Up Breakfast Smoothie, 73
Wassail Bowl, 228
White Sangria, 187, 216
Wine
    Peach Bellinis, 201
    Tropic Ice, 208
    White Sangria, 216
Wow Watermelon Smoothie, 164

METRIC CONVERSION CHART

VOLUME MEASUREMENTS (dry)

1/8 teaspoon = 0.5 mL
1/4 teaspoon = 1 mL
1/2 teaspoon = 2 mL
3/4 teaspoon = 4 mL
1 teaspoon = 5 mL
1 tablespoon = 15 mL
2 tablespoons = 30 mL
1/4 cup = 60 mL
1/3 cup = 75 mL
1/2 cup = 125 mL
2/3 cup = 150 mL
3/4 cup = 175 mL
1 cup = 250 mL
2 cups = 1 pint = 500 mL
3 cups = 750 mL
4 cups = 1 quart = 1 L

VOLUME MEASUREMENTS (fluid)

1 fluid ounce (2 tablespoons) = 30 mL
4 fluid ounces (1/2 cup) = 125 mL
8 fluid ounces (1 cup) = 250 mL
12 fluid ounces (1 1/2 cups) = 375 mL
16 fluid ounces (2 cups) = 500 mL

WEIGHTS (mass)

1/2 ounce = 15 g
1 ounce = 30 g
3 ounces = 90 g
4 ounces = 120 g
8 ounces = 225 g
10 ounces = 285 g
12 ounces = 360 g
16 ounces = 1 pound = 450 g

DIMENSIONS

1/16 inch = 2 mm
1/8 inch = 3 mm
1/4 inch = 6 mm
1/2 inch = 1.5 cm
3/4 inch = 2 cm
1 inch = 2.5 cm

OVEN TEMPERATURES

250°F = 120°C
275°F = 140°C
300°F = 150°C
325°F = 160°C
350°F = 180°C
375°F = 190°C
400°F = 200°C
425°F = 220°C
450°F = 230°C

BAKING PAN SIZES

Utensil	Size in Inches/Quarts	Metric Volume	Size in Centimeters
Baking or	8×8×2	2 L	20×20×5
Cake Pan	9×9×2	2.5 L	23×23×5
(square or	12×8×2	3 L	30×20×5
rectangular)	13×9×2	3.5 L	33×23×5
Loaf Pan	8×4×3	1.5 L	20×10×7
	9×5×3	2 L	23×13×7
Round Layer	8×1½	1.2 L	20×4
Cake Pan	9×1½	1.5 L	23×4
Pie Plate	8×1¼	750 mL	20×3
	9×1¼	1 L	23×3
Baking Dish	1 quart	1 L	—
or Casserole	1½ quart	1.5 L	—
	2 quart	2 L	—